COMPETITIVE

CROSSWORDS

OVER 60 CHALLENGES FROM THE
AMERICAN CROSSWORD PUZZLE TOURNAMENT

Edited by Will Shortz

Andrews McMeel
PUBLISHING®

Andrews McMeel Publishing
a division of Andrews McMeel Universal
1130 Walnut Street, Kansas City, Missouri 64106

www.andrewsmcmeel.com

22 23 24 25 26 RLP 10 9 8 7 6 5 4 3 2 1

ISBN: 978-1-5248-7153-6

Editor: Betty Wong
Art Director: Holly Swayne
Designer: Sierra S. Stanton
Production Editor: Elizabeth A. Garcia
Production Manager: Tamara Haus

CONTENTS

INTRODUCTION

It all began in 1978. One hundred forty-nine crossword lovers and solvers gathered to compete in the first American Crossword Puzzle Tournament. Now, the ACPT—directed by yours truly—has evolved to become the world's oldest and largest crossword event, drawing about a thousand participants each year.

Over the course of two days, solvers race to finish eight original crosswords by leading puzzle constructors. Each crossword has a time limit of 15 to 45 minutes. Competitors earn points for accuracy and speed. The top three contestants go into the championship playoff, solving the final puzzle at large standing boards.

Competitive Crosswords is a collection of 64 puzzles from past ACPTs. Many brilliant crossword constructors contribute their most creative work to the tournament. You'll find some of these clever puzzles in the pages that follow. The crosswords are organized in approximate order of difficulty, with the easiest puzzles at the front and the harder ones toward the back. You can test your speed-solving abilities by following the competition time limits or simply enjoy working these grids at your own pace. Warning: Puzzles on pages 72 through 78 are especially challenging. Don't feel bad if you can't finish them within the time limit, as most contestants don't.

The puzzles in chapter four are playoff puzzles. The clues come in three levels of difficulty: extremely hard ("A"), medium ("B"), and easier ("C"), as marked. The answers are the same in each case. Most people prefer solving with the easier "C" clues, but if you want an extra challenge, start with the "A" clues instead.

The Tournament Play chapter features seven puzzles from the 2014 American Crossword Puzzle Tournament. It is set up so you can score and rank yourself against that year's competitors. If you're curious about how you would finish at an ACPT, solve the puzzles within the given time limits, score yourself using the official rules, and check your ranking. It's almost as good as attending the ACPT in person!

I hope you will enjoy the challenge of this book and consider joining us at the next ACPT.

—Will Shortz

Round 1:
EASY

BLACK AND WHITE by Paula Gamache

It's the principle of the thing.

ACROSS

1 Brazilian dance
6 Sidewalk eatery
10 Gush
14 Police blotter datum
15 Parting words?
16 "Way to go!"
17 Speech difficulties
18 Furious
20 Was indecisive
22 "O Sole ___"
23 Bar mitzvah, e.g.
24 Tough task
28 Baseball's Say Hey Kid
30 Pacific salmon
33 Capri or Elba
34 Touched down
35 Salem's home
37 *Pinafore* letters
38 Depot: Abbr.
39 Opposite principles in this puzzle
40 Super ___ (old video game name)
41 11th-century Spanish hero
42 Boosler of comedy
43 Suffix with annoy
44 Alpha's opposite
46 Itar-___ news agency
47 The "S" of macOS: Abbr.
48 Like most municipal bonds
50 "I could ___ horse!"
52 Superannuated
53 "Out of the question"
57 From head to toe
61 *The ___ Sanction* (Trevanian thriller)
62 Post-shower powder
63 "Go, ___!"
64 Where the action is
65 Very top
66 Collar stiffener
67 Shoulder muscles, for short

DOWN

1 Margarita option
2 "That's ___!" (angry retort)
3 Unemployment rate plus inflation rate
4 Carter or Clinton, religiously
5 Something in the plus column
6 Place for a dock
7 Still sleeping
8 Holiday tree
9 Early sources of modern words
10 Ecclesiastical meetings
11 Baseball throw
12 Corn unit
13 Reporter's question
19 Publicizing
21 Shrink back
24 Navajo dwellings
25 1962 #1 hit by Shelley Fabares
26 Ancient Mexican people
27 Long-eared hound
28 Goat, for Navy
29 Nissan sedan
31 Rococo
32 #1 OutKast hit of 2003
36 Informal request for patience
39 Per annum
43 Dancing Fred
45 It helps keep your feet on the ground
49 Cuts to fit, say
51 In the lead
53 March Madness org.
54 "What's a body to do?!"
55 Penny
56 Notable times
57 Hellenic "H"
58 Little sucker?
59 Stately street liner
60 Bottom line

ENCOURAGING WORDS by Andrea Carla Michaels

A puzzle that provides some figurative pats on the back.

ACROSS

1 Actors Sharif and Epps
6 Battle reminder
10 Inter ___
14 Three trios
15 Pennsylvania port
16 Dozes off
17 "Bravo!"
20 Jacob's twin
21 Alternative to the pill
22 Jack of *The Apartment*
23 Sugar unit
25 Beatles woman with "a little white book"
26 Frighten
28 "Way to go!"
32 Use plastic
33 Figure eight surface
34 Inventor Whitney
35 Mister Ed, for one
36 Publicity
37 See things the same way
39 Lennon's lady
40 Machine with OS
41 Reign of ___
42 "Good job!"
45 Zones
46 Debtors' letters
47 You may put a tree in it
48 Does well on an exam
51 ___ Paolo
52 Certain tide
56 "Take a bow!"
59 Healing plant
60 Israeli airline
61 Green pasta sauce
62 [Bo-o-oring!]
63 More than serious
64 Really bother

DOWN

1 T. H. White's *The ___ and Future King*
2 Cattle calls
3 ___ *Karenina*
4 People a bartender recognizes
5 Orchestra sect.
6 Arrange
7 "Rats!"
8 Be under the weather
9 Come to understand
10 Alternative to vegetable or mineral
11 Weaving machine
12 "___ idea!"
13 Guild: Abbr.
18 Singer Mann
19 French bean
24 Not just suggest
25 Pool ball holder
26 Glowed like the sun
27 "O Little Town of Bethlehem," e.g.
28 Chop finely
29 ___ firma
30 Margarines
31 Zwei + zwei
32 Camp food
36 Writer Fleming and others
37 Pilot's prefix
38 Japanese beverage
40 Sassed, with "off"
41 Nevada/California lake
43 Lend an ear
44 "Stop dawdling!"
47 Luxurious fur
48 "An apple ___ . . ."
49 Pepsi or RC
50 Sufficient, in poetry
51 One with top billing
53 Toward sunrise
54 Neighbor of Sask.
55 Scheme
57 Rumble in the Jungle victor
58 Imitate

ARMS RACE by Byron Walden

Starting off with a bang!

ACROSS

1. 44th US president
6. Music groups
11. Homer Simpson exclamation
14. The "L" in LEM
15. Run ___ of (cross)
16. Time in history
17. Listlessness
18. ___ rays
19. Feb. preceder
20. Really on a roll
23. Persian or Abyssinian
24. "Don we now our ___ apparel"
25. Suit material
26. "So sad!"
28. Builder's instructions, briefly
32 & 33. 26th Amendment beneficiary
35. Los ___ National Laboratory
37. Extremely nervous
42. Progresso soup variety
43. Andrea ___ (ill-fated ship)
44. Flaky mineral
47. Ed who starred on Lou Grant
49. Bird's name after house or Carolina
50. Pointless
52. "Would I do such a thing?"
54. Opposite of subtract
55. "Without a doubt!"
60. Funerary container
61. Quick
62. Name badge
64. Envision
65. Barter
66. Desmond of Sunset Boulevard
67. Sinuous curve
68. Area in a sultan's palace, once
69. So far

DOWN

1. Corrida cry
2. Small house with a porch
3. Comment on, as in the margin
4. Home to Kahului Airport
5. "Give me ___" ("Call sometime")
6. Cargos, for example
7. Way off yonder
8. Seward Peninsula city
9. Russian parliament
10. Bed frame pieces
11. By law: Lat.
12. California county whose seat is Santa Ana
13. Actress Balaban
21. Tank filler
22. Almost runs out of juice, as a battery
23. Cleveland cagers
27. Ship's route
29. ___ Marbles (sculptures at the British Museum)
30. Means of Internet access
31. Home of the George W. Bush Presidential Lib.
34. Hwy.
36. Antiquated
38. Put ___ good word for
39. Knightly activity
40. Precursor of overtime
41. Hourglass contents
44. Ignore the instructions for
45. Accustoms
46. Kim with the 1981 #1 hit "Bette Davis Eyes"
48. Kanga's kid
51. Our planet
53. Singer Turner's autobiography
56. Two Mules for Sister ___
57. Practice boxing
58. Seek's partner
59. Altar exchange
63. Gangster's rod

4

FLIP-FLOPS by Stanley Newman

It's the same, and yet different.

TIME LIMIT | YOUR TIME
15 MINUTES |

ACROSS

1 Moves without a foot on the accelerator
7 Pet welfare org.
11 "No ___" (food spec)
14 Ultimate result
15 Future atty.'s hurdle
16 Federal org. with a flower logo
17 Lionel Richie Oscar-winning song
19 Five-digit number, in brief
20 Frequent February forecast
21 Suffix with exist
22 Letter after wye
23 With 52-Across, part of a wedding day rhyme
27 Accompaniment to a Native American dance
30 ". . . ___ iron bars a cage"
31 Org. in the health care debate
32 Place to learn CPR
36 Hindi "master"
40 Not necessarily
44 Certain golf tourney
45 Org. fighting street gangs
46 Football linemen: Abbr.
47 Medic's bag
49 Collectable 1950s cars
52 See 23-Across
58 Quid pro ___
59 Jacob's twin
60 Sides of a doorway
64 Half of dos
65 Reliably and consistently
67 Hotshot aviator
68 Swashbuckler's challenge
69 Disinclined
70 Turner who founded CNN
71 B'way buys
72 Least genteel

DOWN

1 "Ornery" guy
2 Australia's national gemstone
3 "___ sow, so shall . . ."
4 Most timid
5 Artificially elegant
6 Fellow in an RV?
7 Point of view
8 Defeat through mind games, with "out"
9 Arrived
10 Supped
11 Operatic voice, for short
12 Sales pitch
13 Opened wide
18 Get the point of
24 Credit card exp. date format
25 Likely to pry
26 Seize
27 Push (down)
28 Actor Sharif
29 Bread spread
33 Oscar/Emmy/Tony/Grammy winner Brooks
34 Letters on some Civil War belt buckles
35 Increase, with "up"
37 Roll-call response
38 Part of IHOP: Abbr.
39 One in charge
41 Swelter
42 Give off
43 Port of Yemen
48 Aptly named journal of the American Ornithologists' Union
50 Feeling of familiarity
51 Convinced
52 Lower body exercise
53 About 28 grams
54 Spoke with a Jersey accent?
55 "The best ___ to come"
56 Gets exactly right
57 Race starter's aid
61 Additional amount
62 Smooch
63 Proofreader's mark
65 Banned insecticide
66 Patriotic women's org.

BLITHE SPIRIT by Kelly Clark

An easy, breezy puzzle designed to get you off to a fast start.

ACROSS

1 Aerobic exercise popularized by Billy Blanks
6 Island with the Blue Grotto
11 Butcher, baker, or candlestick maker
14 Like a big brother
15 Schoolroom with microprocessors
16 It's mined
17 Hot-button issue of 2000s politics
19 Young fellow
20 Like most hospital inspections
21 Use a shovel
22 Woes
23 NYC neighborhood west of the East Village
25 Peevish
27 Sequels often have them in their titles
31 Disney septet
34 Sugar suffix
35 USMC noncoms
37 Homecoming parade project
38 "Yeah, why not"
40 One of the 31-Across
42 Amorous stare
43 Premature
45 Dresses for ranis
47 U-turn from WNW
48 Paris palace
50 Vacillated
52 Removes from a mother's milk
54 Carrier with a six-point star on its jets
55 Parisian pals
57 Invitation reply facilitator, for short
59 Composer Shostakovich
63 Guided
64 One way to prepare eggs
66 Paid athlete
67 Squabble
68 Spanish kids
69 Wrap (up)
70 Pre-1917 Russian rulers
71 The Jetsons' dog

DOWN

1 Like many a fast-food order
2 Alda of *M*A*S*H*
3 Ice cream brand
4 Words on a Valentine candy heart
5 Keynote givers
6 EMT's skill
7 Etcher's fluid
8 Braid
9 Trash-talked, with "on"
10 "Where would ___ without you?"
11 Pirate's ensign
12 Not written
13 Flower plots
18 Discuss yet again
22 Author Calvino
24 Gymnast Korbut and others
26 Inits. in a personal ad
27 "Long time ___!"
28 Same old
29 Lehár operetta, with "The"
30 March 17 honoree, for short
32 Not so
33 Spirited mount
36 Crazed shopper's outing
39 Somebody ___ (not yours)
41 Gives the right of way
44 Nay's opposite
46 Endurance
49 Subsequently happens
51 Slurs over
53 Yuletide figure
55 Swiss range
56 Nothing more than
58 ___'acte
60 Camper's shelter
61 Regretful one
62 ___ facto
64 Former flier
65 Slangy greetings

PLUS TEN by Lynn Lempel

An exercise in simple addition.

ACROSS

1 Quick punches in the ring
5 Painter Picasso
10 On
14 Replacement for the lira and mark
15 Editor's insertion mark
16 Famed Roman "fiddler"
17 Worker's brief cry of relief
18 Addition to the Superdome in New Orleans?
20 Cars sporting four rings
22 One might make you cry "59-Across!"
23 Mount Everest?
26 Enticed
29 Tee preceder
30 Señor's "that"
31 Had a feeling about
32 Actor Eli of *The Good, the Bad and the Ugly*
35 Bake-off entry, perhaps
36 Arrive wearing a skin-tight getup?
38 It goes out with the Tide
40 Motors
41 Parody
43 Hamm on a soccer field
44 "Toodle-oo!"
47 Shimmery cloth
48 Give Trebek a drubbing?
51 Total
53 Melting snow
54 Costly carved watch?
58 Cookbook compiler Rombauer
59 See 22-Across
60 Herb used in making absinthe
61 Asia's shrunken ___ Sea
62 Lunch orders, briefly
63 Religious subgroups
64 "Auld Lang ___"

DOWN

1 Period noted for a sharp increase in globalization
2 Bodes
3 Ones ending their engagements?
4 Bulgaria's capital
5 Dell products, for short
6 Hotel-rating org.
7 Payment from a palm greaser
8 Big name in tableware
9 Name of four Holy Roman emperors
10 Proclaims publicly
11 Instrument for Stan Getz or John Coltrane
12 Buried treasure of sorts
13 Word after small or chicken
19 Competent
21 Power source for early locomotives
24 Catching some Z's
25 Sarah depicted in *Game Change*
27 "Yow!"
28 Gen. who became a pres.
31 Grammy winner Twain
32 Prolixity
33 Lee who won an Oscar for *Brokeback Mountain*
34 Weather conditions, poetically
36 Disdain
37 Pirates and Buccaneers
38 CIA forerunner
39 Antinarcotic org.
42 "Render ____ Caesar . . ."
44 Out of focus
45 Compliant type
46 Breathe out
48 Old hag
49 Thing from the past
50 Assumed name
52 Some nest eggs, in brief
54 Corn waste
55 "You've got mail" ISP
56 Superlative suffix
57 Adult movies get three of them

BUZZ WORDS by Lynn Lempel

For an easy puzzle, this challenge is surprisingly stiff.

ACROSS

1 Bumbling
6 Part of PTA: Abbr.
10 Historian's purview
14 Film feature once Dorothy gets to Oz
15 Cook some cookies, say
16 ___ la Douce
17 College course that covers the classics, colloquially
19 Cause to stumble
20 "Of course!"
21 Ballerina's support
22 Large amount
23 Hula accompaniment, for short
24 Subtropical weather system in the Atlantic
27 Eat like a bird
29 Harrison who played Professor Higgins
30 Earth-related prefix
31 Earth
32 Hourly pay
34 Prince Charles's sister
35 Some offensive linemen . . . or what 17-, 24-, 49- and 58-Across could be said to have?
38 Ben-Hur setting
41 Clumsy sorts
42 People who cry foul
45 Formula ___ (type of auto racing)
46 Retail tycoon Walton
47 Find out about
49 Situation that might lead to a grand slam
53 Suffix with magnet or quartz
54 Hawke of Dead Poets Society
55 PETA taboo
56 Tennis trailblazer on a 37¢ stamp
57 Trounce
58 Attacked with incendiary devices
61 Julius Caesar garment
62 Superstar, to fans
63 Tractor name
64 "Immediately!"
65 Head honcho
66 Twisted smile

DOWN

1 Freezes over
2 Chant outside a modern power plant, maybe
3 Spanish painter known for his elongated figures
4 Barber's striped attention-getter
5 Prefix with cycle
6 Detest
7 Massachusetts town with a witch museum
8 Compete in the giant slalom, e.g.
9 Earn as profit
10 Sales spiel
11 Summon to court to answer a charge
12 Teensy amount
13 One of a pair for Astaire
18 "Keep it," to a proofreader
22 Lisa Simpson's instrument, for short
24 Neighbor of Java
25 Impulses
26 Bestselling cookbook author Paula
28 Toy on a string
32 Company that makes 43-Downs
33 Org. that hunts smugglers
34 On the briny
36 Soccer score
37 1857's ___ Scott decision
38 Key Supreme Court vote upholding the Affordable Care Act
39 Bingeing
40 Off one's rocker, to a yenta
43 Toy used in disc golf
44 "I showed you!"
46 Nine-digit ID
47 Parsley or basil
48 Backyard bird enticement
50 Trouble persistently
51 Some natural dos
52 Confrontations at 20 paces, say
56 Grace finale
58 "Oh, I loved your fruitcake," maybe
59 Wedding words
60 Takes too much, briefly

MAKING A LIST by Mike Shenk

You've got some unfinished business.

ACROSS

1 Wait, as one's time
5 Boutique
9 Temporarily do the job of
14 Nasdaq alternative
15 Cedar Rapids's home
16 Maker of the first move
17 Go to natural history museum to check out . . .
19 It arches over the heart
20 Built up over time
21 Treacherous sort
23 Set the price at
24 Choreographer de Mille
25 Rewrite business plan so viability isn't . . .
30 Considerably
31 Robert Burns, for one
32 Wild
34 Numbered work
36 One-time retail giant with more than 2,000 stores
39 Its motto is "Lux et Veritas"
40
42 Lab warning
44 ___ populi
45 Learn history of Hispaniola from friend who is . . .
49 Personal record
50 "Luck ___ Lady Tonight"
51 Cow chow
54 1968 film with a famous car chase
58 Had in mind
59 Clean fridge to get rid of . . .
61 In reserve
62 Scheherazade offering
63 Fair feature
64 Like shoes
65 Bats one's gums
66 Tycoons often have big ones

DOWN

1 Bear Bryant's team, familiarly
2 Computer originally offered in Bondi Blue
3 Genealogy abbr.
4 Much of an epic movie's cast
5 Robin, to Batman
6 Rain poncho part
7 To each his ___
8 Earn $200, in a way
9 Familiar with
10 Faux Chinese dish
11 Potential swing
12 Bus. letter heading
13 Airplane assignment
18 Gives the boot
22 Coda
24 Encouraging utterance
25 Attire for the Headless Horseman and others
26 Island whose capital is Oranjestad
27 Montreal moniker
28 Cheer for the diva
29 Hawk's grasper
30 Gift tag word
33 ___ Luthor of *Superman*
35 Annual film festival site
37 Fleecy father
38 Protectors of people's rights
41 Overly formal
43 Prepared to be knighted
46 Big palooka
47 Admitting air currents
48 In abundance
51 Shepherd with an Old Testament book named for him
52 Former name in late-night
53 Go bankrupt
54 Take in
55 Hepcat's words of understanding
56 Agenda hidden in 17-, 25-, 45-, and 59-Across
57 Spain : muy :: France : ____
60 Highest bond rating

CAN YOU DIG IT? by Paula Gamache

Something you have to understand . . .

ACROSS

1 Other than this
5 Passion
9 Clobber
14 Spreadsheet box
15 Parade entrance, maybe
16 It's between Quebec and Sierra in a phonetic alphabet
17 Track shape
18 North-flowing river of Africa
19 Public persona
20 Digs
23 Western treaty grp.
24 Tabloid bit
25 Digs
32 Clerical vestment
33 ___'acte
34 Arizona Red Rock Country locale
35 Period of prosperity
37 Scenery chewer
39 "Yikes!"
40 Except if
43 Somme silk
46 First family member
47 Digs
50 Appear to be
51 Where It. is
52 Digs
59 Nitpick
60 Sniffer
61 You can buy things online with this
62 Valuable violin
63 Major addition?
64 Peeling potatoes, say, in the military
65 Thick as a brick
66 Israeli prime minister during the Yom Kippur War
67 Capone nemesis

DOWN

1 Tree hugger's interest: Abbr.
2 ___ Strauss jeans
3 Belarussian, e.g.
4 Singing partner of Doherty, Phillips, and Phillips
5 Doesn't give up the fight
6 La Salle of *ER*
7 Org. that defends equal protection
8 Something good to clear
9 Request from a pen pal
10 Not store-bought
11 Poet ___ Khayyám
12 RAM units
13 "Once upon a midnight dreary . . ." writer
21 ___ the Great (boy detective)
22 Itinerary nos.
25 Exact copy
26 Letter-shaped fastener
27 Utmost
28 Understand
29 "Understood"
30 Scoundrel
31 Marquis name
32 "Snug as ___ . . ."
36 Portable sets of utensils
38 Coy reply from Miss Piggy
41 Metal marble
42 "___ Gone" (Hall & Oates hit)
44 Brew produced at subfreezing temperatures
45 Decorative needle case
48 *The Marshall Mathers LP* rapper
49 Encourage
52 Ineffectual, as an attempt
53 *Ghostbusters* director Reitman
54 E, G, B, D, or F
55 Piedmont wine center
56 Lose power
57 Inquires
58 Informal affirmatives
59 No-goodnik

TWICE AS NICE
by Andrea Carla Michaels and Myles Callum

You'll have to spell it out for us, please.

ACROSS

1 Headline?
5 Hay storage site
9 Move like Jell-O
14 One who regrets
15 Kazan who directed *Gentlemen's Agreement*
16 Caught wrigglers
17 It cuts both ways
20 Like the king in *The King and I*
21 Place to get gas?
22 Star turns
23 What buffalo of song do
24 Washer cycle
27 Cash in, as a coupon
32 '50s prez
35 Stir up
37 Ticklish Muppet
38 London transport
42 Frozen waffle brand
43 Fine gown material
44 Kind of blonde
45 Give, as homework
48 Collette, Morrison, and Braxton
50 Fireworks sounds?
52 The Gees of the Bee Gees
56 Gorged oneself
60 Warm and having a light breeze, maybe
62 Large mobile home
64 "Li'l" cartoon character
65 Author Koontz
66 Jai ___
67 Prepared
68 Pharaoh ___ (pests)
69 Scratch

10 Chopped down
11 Medicinal plant
12 *The King and I* costar
13 It tends to go counterclockwise in the Northern Hemisphere
18 Yen
19 ___ Abby
23 Ushers to a better row, perhaps
25 Neither's partner
26 Cheap beer
28 ___ *Rosenkavalier*
29 "Able was I ere I saw ___"
30 Stock on an Australian ranch

31 Get into the hits at a rock concert?
32 "The very ___!"
33 26-Down dispensers
34 E.R. tests
36 Prefix with plasm
39 Fish in an ornamental pond
40 Relatives
41 Big question mark
46 Err
47 Response to the Little Red Hen
49 Apelike
51 Gossipy Hopper
53 Beautiful, in Verona
54 Moolah

55 Mount Hermon is its highest peak
56 Man ___
57 Groovy feeling
58 Dame ___ (Barry Humphries role)
59 Bamboo, e.g.
60 RBI or HR
61 Coffee holders
63 Dark time, in poetry

DOWN

1 Iron
2 Radio feed
3 Fit for a queen
4 Aftershock
5 Bottom of the barrel
6 Ye ___ Curiosity Shoppe
7 Adam and Eve's tree?
8 Karate-like exercise
9 Bagel choice

WITHOUT FAIL by Mike Nothnagel

A puzzle with a common end.

ACROSS

1 Gridiron datum
5 Commit a gridiron infraction
9 Waits expectantly
14 Unloading site
15 Top of the heap
16 Son of Cain
17 *1989 John Candy comedy
19 Veep between Hubert and Gerald
20 Goddess whose helmet is on the US Military Academy's coat of arms
21 Consumed
23 "Ta-ta!"
24 Spanish article
26 "Nuts!"
27 *Military pooh-bah
30 "Piggy"
33 "Holy moly!"
36 Wine glass part
37 Commenting on an ongoing winning streak, some say
38 "Amo, amas, ___ . . ."
39 Shrek princess
40 Send off
41 "Something's gotta ___"
42 Speller's specification
43 Decade after the '00s
44 Grunts may come from it
45 *Place to buy a smoothie
47 Fed
49 Mythical bird
50 Commercial suffix with Power
53 Announcement of one's arrival
56 Totally lose it
58 Online commerce center
59 *Tool with a flame
62 Flood protection
63 On ___ (without thinking)
64 Man's name that's almost a homophone of 63-Across
65 Something with a circular window, maybe
66 Trash boat
67 What you can do to the end of the answer to each starred clue

DOWN

1 Dinner fowl
2 Familial nickname
3 Hidden supply
4 Actor MacLachlan
5 Poolside structure
6 Mary's boss on The Mary Tyler Moore Show
7 Magazine with an annual "500" list
8 Pug-nosed pooch
9 Most skilled in
10 How a confident solver may solve a crossword
11 *Serving a sentence
12 Beige alternative
13 Boutique
18 Accustom
22 Battlestar Galactica commander
25 Pilgrimage site for many Italians
27 Put some teeth into?
28 Seneca or Cato the Younger
29 Marilu of Taxi
31 "Come ___!" ("The door's open!")
32 Tel. no. additions
33 Veers back sharply
34 Skip
35 *Woodstock emcee who had a Ben & Jerry's flavor named after him
37 Derisive shout
39 Local wildlife
43 Implied, as an agreement
45 Key person?
46 Dog, in kiddie-talk
48 Small riot
50 It comes from the heart
51 Air passages
52 Community's shared values
53 Clung to
54 Part of EMT: Abbr.
55 Entrepreneurs' degs.
57 Sticky stuff
60 Jean-___ Picard of Star Trek
61 Oklahoma native

A UN ASSEMBLY
by Bonnie L. Gentry and Victor Fleming

A challenge that's not too daunting.

TIME LIMIT	YOUR TIME
20 MINUTES	

ACROSS

1 Sugar's partner
6 Dessert with ice cream
11 Valentine's Day mo.
14 Hi, in Hilo
15 Available
16 Home on the Web
17 Gathering of big wheels to christen a ship?
19 ___ Maria
20 Exchange words (with)
21 1776 and 2001: Abbr.
22 Catcher's position
24 Alliance of 1958–61: Abbr.
26 D-Day time
27 Eerily disturbing to an Updike protagonist?
33 Androphobiacs' fear
34 Movie word before Eleven, Twelve, or Thirteen
35 "Understood"
36 Put an ___
38 Chip in
39 Rock genre
40 Eyelid annoyance
41 Cast on the road?
43 "___ a beautiful day for a crossword tournament"
44 Result of eating at too many luaus?
47 Selling point
48 Mail ctr.
49 Preserves, e.g.
51 Cry of discovery
53 Amts. of cooking oil, e.g.
57 "Say again?"
58 "Goatlike deity? I don't think so!"?
61 "Te ___ Corazón" (2005 Prince single)
62 Male pitching woo
63 What one is expert in
64 Guy's date
65 Students taking Torts or Contracts, say
66 Done to death

DOWN

1 Easy marks
2 Raindrop sound
3 Where Red Delicious apples originated
4 Little angel
5 Exaggerated feature in an Obama cartoon
6 Beast that slew Adonis
7 Major load
8 K2, for one: Abbr.
9 God of revelry and wine
10 Nora who wrote and directed *Julie & Julia*
11 Forward-looking
12 Guitarist Clapton
13 Hardly electrifying
18 Words
23 Convex button
25 Peek-___
26 Deliver, as an indictment
27 Designer Oscar de la ___
28 Who once said "I am a deeply superficial person"
29 Attack with vigor
30 Wore
31 "___ the spreading chestnut tree"
32 Comes together
33 Get engaged?
37 Make frizzy, as hair
39 "You crack ___!"
41 Secure firmly
42 Polytheist
45 Parental words following "because"
46 Against
49 Layered hairdo
50 Rockies predator
51 Seed case
52 Certain lobsters
54 Goa garment
55 When repeated, mini-golf
56 Weapon in *The Mikado*
59 Fed. that includes Dubai
60 A lot, to a poet

TWO FOR THE SHOW by Ian Livengood

Some pairs of films we'd like to see share a marquee.

ACROSS

1 Early Chevy hybrid
5 Tent, sleeping bag, etc.
9 Heroic tales
14 Arabian kingpin
15 Bar under a car
16 Banishment
17 Himalayan priest
18 What 15-Acrosses do
19 Upscale watch brand
20 Group on trial after the 1968 Democratic National Convention [2002, 1995]
23 Risqué or violent, say
24 Two-screen theater
25 Morning beverages, informally
28 Carry-___
29 Jar topper
31 Hit the accelerator [1994, 2009]
33 Radner of *Saturday Night Live*
35 ___ *Lisa*
36 Old-fashioned theater offering . . . or a hint to 20-, 31-, 43- and 56-Across
41 The Red Planet
42 Ones learning the ropes
43 Excessive styling result [1988, 1979]
47 Flight board posting, for short
48 Part of ACC: Abbr.
51 Total jerk
52 Cocktail party cheese
54 "I'll say!"
56 "Yield" and "Stop" [2000, 2002]
58 Month before agosto
61 Miller ___
62 "No way, Boris"
63 Scent
64 Brio
65 Charles Lamb, to readers
66 Kind of metaphor
67 Editor's mark
68 Shipped

DOWN

1 Buttonless fastener
2 Certain Cornhusker
3 Restricts
4 Slightest residue
5 Patio apparatus that may have a tank
6 Trade show
7 Like top celebrities
8 Doesn't let lapse
9 Tranquil
10 Nerve impulse conductor
11 Hodges of baseball
12 Pub pint
13 The birds and the bees
21 Speak off the cuff
22 Red carpet walker, informally
25 Scent
26 Flag Day month
27 Place to get a mani-pedi
30 '50s Oval Office inits.
32 Outback runners
33 Speak effusively
34 Rearward at sea
36 Stand for an emcee
37 Assns.
38 John Wayne had one in *True Grit*
39 Gallery world
40 Hurly-burlies
41 Financier's deg.
44 Out of the country
45 Lyricist Gershwin
46 Ransacked and robbed
48 Sock pattern
49 Get a program on the radio
50 Anne Rice vampire
53 Submit online forms
55 Trident parts
56 Proctor's call
57 Slanted, in a way: Abbr.
58 Smucker's product
59 Spoon-bending Geller
60 Bagel topping

IMMORTAL COMBAT by Ian Livengood

The circled letters provide a clue to what's hidden in the three long Across answers.

ACROSS

1 Texas city where Dr Pepper originated
5 Honcho
9 Bicker
13 ___ about (roughly)
14 Declaration made with chips
16 Melodic subject, in music
17 Mean beast
18 Short part
19 Pet food giant
20 Protection for coastal homes
23 Poetic contraction
24 Swap rings
25 Tourist guide listings
27 President who was once a union leader
29 Isle of Man resident
31 John F. Kennedy Library architect
32 They may be holy or marching
34 Lords and masters
35 Nations providing cradle-to-grave programs
39 ___-Frank Act of 2010
40 Delaware tribe
41 Item on a mantel
42 Pilgrimage, maybe
44 Japanese loungewear
48 "My sentiments exactly"
50 Political rival of D.D.E.
51 The Rockets, on scoreboards
52 They start at the first grade
56 It might be drawn at night
57 Fight site
58 Not one ___
59 1847 adventure novel
60 Green Party candidate of 2000
61 Memo
62 ___ pool
63 Put to sleep, say
64 Migratory food fish

DOWN

1 Low speaker
2 *Life of Pi* director
3 Dos Equis rival
4 Mega Stuf cookie
5 Spread south of the border
6 Horned African beast
7 Poor offerings
8 "Mon ___!"
9 Police setup
10 Fruity dessert baked in a pan
11 Electric gauges
12 Dorm VIPs
15 Like the name hidden in 20-Across
21 *The Hobbit* figure
22 Have a bug
26 Family nickname
28 First-place medal
29 Like the name hidden in 35-Across
30 One "A" in MPAA: Abbr.
33 Writer ___ Stanley Gardner
34 Petiole's place
35 Boggle, e.g.
36 *The Honeymooners* wacky neighbor
37 Parting phrase
38 Silly
39 Motorist's offense, for short
42 ___ Haverford, *Parks and Recreation* character
43 Like the name hidden in 52-Across
45 "Call on me! I've got it!"
46 Big Apple area west of the Bowery
47 Expelled
49 Lake between two western states
50 Santa's player in *Elf*, 2003
53 Speedy steed
54 Overhaul
55 Holds
56 Swamp

Solving in progress

Wordle creator, Josh Wardle, with Will Shortz

Color commentary by composer Greg Pliska
and comedian Ophira Eisenberg

Round 2:
MEDIUM

WHAT ARE THEY? by Maura Jacobson

Fictional people and what they stand for.

ACROSS

1 Langley Field, e.g.: Abbr.
4 Unkosher
8 Goes bad
12 Fen-___, former diet drug combo
16 Move, in realtor lingo
18 "Present"
19 Suffix with switch
20 Tug-of-war need
21 Thomas Vandyke
23 Elaine Rose
25 Naked
26 Continental money
28 Played for time
29 Igloo dweller: Abbr.
30 Natalie Stack
33 Spacewalk, for short
34 Makes a run for it
36 Abigail McIntosh
41 Poker declaration
43 They may be blue
46 Boozehound
47 Did a glissade
48 Oliver Post
51 HS dropout's goal
52 Throw
53 Gumshoe's hat
54 Globe Theatre villain
56 ___ out a living
58 Hankering
59 Ezra Silver
63 14+
66 Motorist's caution
67 Spanish direction
68 Window decor
72 Football Hall of Fame coach George
74 Mouse catcher
76 Thomas Fellows
78 Kind of mitt
79 Seattle-to-Phoenix dir.
80 "Little" boy of the comics
81 Irving's *A Prayer for ___ Meany*
82 Edith Romano
85 Title for Macbeth

88 Procter & Gamble detergent
89 Geena Stein
92 On a pension: Abbr.
95 Highway exit
99 Star quality
100 Hoi polloi
102 Robert Peck
104 Lucille Chambers
106 Chess cry
107 The hots
108 Peace Nobelist Wiesel
109 Celt
110 ___ collar
111 Annual athletic award
112 Changed to redhead, e.g.
113 La-la lead-in

DOWN

1 Bicker
2 Bouquet fronds
3 Karen Crane
4 Exactly, after "on"
5 Stephen of *The Crying Game*
6 Was in the wrong
7 Disgusted
8 Cast over
9 ___ pro nobis
10 Dolls and balls
11 Most cushy
12 Slip out of place
13 Wolf's call
14 Relative of a rapier
15 Dweeb
17 Olive ___
22 Cry like a baby
24 Kind of flow
27 River inlets
31 Accords site of 1993
32 Relieve tightness
35 Winning
37 Runway walker
38 Dramatist's work
39 Not on tape
40 *Paradise Lost* setting

41 To laugh or to cry: Abbr.
42 Larry and Curly's partner
44 "Put ___ on it!"
45 Sneaky sort
49 ___ Perot
50 Drake of *Perry Mason*
51 *Faust* poet
52 Classic wordless comic
55 Sporty cars, for short
57 17th-century pirate captain
60 Choker
61 Paper quantity
62 Neighbor of Cameroon
63 "Whoops!"
64 Eat
65 Something found in a lab coat
69 Tyrone Craft
70 Hurricane center
71 Nine-digit ID
73 "The Ugly Duckling" writer
75 Herbicide target
77 Campus military grp.
79 Walk lazily
80 St. Petersburg's river
83 Suffix with theo-
84 Football score
86 Pitched
87 On ___ with
90 Plant securely: Var.
91 SpringFree maker
93 Elsie the Cow's mate
94 Rival of Edison
95 "For the life ___ . . ."
96 Campus digs
97 Pic
98 ___ XII, 1939–58
101 Swamp
103 Recipe amt.
105 "The dog ate my homework," probably

ELMER FUDDISMS by Maura Jacobson

As in . . . be vewwwy, vewwwy quiet!

ACROSS

1 Wear away by rubbing
7 Phony
11 Winters' falls
16 Truck engine
17 Seat of Allen County, Kan.
18 Peeved
20 Part of SSN
21 Taunting simile for an obese person?
23 Old Icelandic literary work
24 Magna ___ laude
25 "Naughty!"
26 Repeated call in a dance class
27 Pepe the cartoon skunk
29 Unborn twins?
32 Recipe meas.
33 Cereal bit
34 The same as above
36 Append
37 Hypotheticals
39 Succumbed to submersion
41 Geisha's sash
43 Item for a TV *Roadshow*
47 Infuriate
48 Pursue stealthily
50 Reddish-brown
51 Devilish
53 Scottish John
55 Sixth word of the Gettysburg Address
56 Below
59 Croquet player's ailment?
61 Charon's destination
63 Writer Santha Rama ___
64 Matterhorn, for one
65 Divorce
67 Kind of plane
70 Tiffs
72 Compass part
76 Home of ancient Sparta
78 Yes at sea
79 Better prepared
80 Markham's "The Man with the ___"
81 Motivator for a lazybones
83 One twixt 12 and 20

84 "My gal" of song
85 US dance co.
87 Underside of a pan?
91 Stingless bee
93 Bryn ___
95 Workers' advocate at the UN
96 With "on" plus 9-Down, exposed to risk
97 Twist
98 Story about an unemployed hag?
101 *Dallas* family
104 Grammy winner Wonder and others
105 Birthday serving
106 Very last part
107 Have the wheel
108 Something ___
109 Caste members

DOWN

1 Classifieds, e.g.
2 Life story, briefly
3 Stimulus responder
4 Covert stage comment
5 Bygone bird?
6 Singing Fitzgerald
7 Laugh track runner
8 Boring
9 See 96-Across
10 "Whew!"
11 Plumber's tool
12 SSE's opposite
13 Cries at a circus
14 Earp posse?
15 Tennis's Monica
18 #2 prosecutor: Abbr.
19 Johnny of *Pirates of the Caribbean*
22 Not much
27 Miner's bonanza
28 Get deservedly
29 Good day to get married?: Abbr.
30 Post
31 In ___ (as found)

35 Adjudge
38 Taradiddle
40 Ford a stream, maybe
41 Ear-related
42 Boston neighborhood
44 Bert Bobbsey's twin
45 Feel the ___
46 900+ year-old son of 97-Down
48 Quick scissor strokes
49 Toys with tails
52 Harry Potter's pet bird
54 ___ rule (generally)
56 Russia's ___ Mountains
57 Rocketeer's acronym
58 Chirping sound in Holland?
60 Art Deco master
61 Clamor heard on an Asian river?
62 Imitated
64 Louisville's ___ Center
66 Body part with a cap
68 Kanga's child
69 All over again
71 Half a Samoan capital
73 Like a black sheep, maybe
74 Tilt
75 Halliburton of the Halliburton company
77 Places for shackles
79 Dream phase, for short
82 *Baby, Take ___* (Shirley Temple film)
83 "Nearer My God ___"
85 Quantities: Abbr.
86 Bangkok coins
88 Ship of fuels
89 Not just damage
90 Covers snugly, with "in"
92 Occupy the throne
94 Rend
97 Son after Cain and Abel
99 Not survive
100 The rocks in "on the rocks"
102 Wildebeest
103 '60s coll. radicals

SWITCHEROO by Maura Jacobson

Calling Rev. Spooner and all his relatives.

ACROSS

1 Diaper wearer
5 Highest peak in the Philippines
10 Dance move
14 Pilgrimage
17 Surrounding glow
18 Love to bits
19 Capital of Italia
20 The Sun Devils of the PAC-12: Abbr.
21 Put all the kings' seats below deck?
24 Nancy Drew's boyfriend
25 Shakespeare volume
26 Suffix with elephant
27 Time off from work
29 TV's warrior princess
30 German's one
32 Hall of Fame shortstop Aparicio
33 Mother-of-pearl
35 Dweeb's favorite Campbell's product?
40 Biblical verb ending
41 Walked (on)
43 Big elephant feature
44 All there
45 Row makers
47 New York city on the Mohawk
50 Football pickup
53 "Ka-blam!"
54 Syrup used as an emetic
56 They may be left running at a stand
58 Madres' brothers
60 Astronaut's dessert bonanza?
64 Like so
65 Actor Morales
66 Bobcats
69 Male clotheshorse
72 Exxon, formerly
74 Toastmaster
76 Neutral shade
77 Adjoin
79 She never had a mother

81 Ingrid's *Casablanca* role
83 Whopper
84 Outcry when a pizza is cut unevenly?
89 Determined's partner
91 "Get ___ writing"
92 Sisters with habits
93 Gangland guns
94 Italian rice dish
97 Ventilate
98 Job before a film is shot
101 Bonn cry of woe
102 Bread-maker's massive slicer?
105 Coffee, slangily
106 Golden rule word
107 Chutzpah
108 Have on
109 Most-used conjunction
110 For fear that
111 Assassinated
112 Sacred serpents of Egypt

DOWN

1 What Paul McCartney played in the Beatles
2 A plane may be on it
3 Raspberry
4 Big bore
5 Conductor Zubin
6 Men in a tub?
7 Start of a volume 1
8 Weaker
9 Log-in system for multiple sites
10 Lady of Mex.
11 Takes to a garage, say
12 Sends with a click
13 Raise's opposite
14 Lava, e.g.
15 Like men in a tub?
16 Judge ___
22 Belief
23 Detect
28 X, on a letter
31 Site with a "Buy It Now" option

33 Classic brand of pop
34 Covering
35 "___ on your life!"
36 Decree
37 Bard's Muse
38 Game with a 108-card deck
39 Hymnal spot
42 Commotion
46 Kiltie
48 Bistro
49 Rough up
51 Shoulder firearms
52 Lamebrained
55 Feel muscle-sore
57 Ambitious bridge bid
59 ___ qua non
61 German steel city
62 Permissible
63 TV news coups
67 "___ go bragh!"
68 Made a case of it
69 Temporary "in" thing
70 Geisha's waistband
71 Gave detention, e.g.
73 Stove compartment
75 Bridge whiz Culbertson
78 Dog that went to Oz
80 Of the same rank
82 Reduce in rank
85 Uneasy, as sleep
86 Chant
87 Groups with dues
88 Neighbor of Lebanon
90 Parliament site in North America
93 Ancient Greek physician
94 Hindu prince
95 Computer symbol
96 Excuses
98 AD 206
99 Half-moon tide
100 Dogs' snarls
103 Go bad
104 Title for Angelico

MISFILINGS by Maura Jacobson

Seemingly, the new library assistant hasn't a clue.

ACROSS

1. Encountered
4. NYC sports venue
7. Historian's subject
11. Library holding misfiled under ANIMAL SOUNDS
15. Sound rebound
17. Silents star Naldi
18. Not fooled by
19. Hawkeye State
20. Miners' quests
21. Something it's not good to put off
22. Rebounds per game, e.g.
23. Relative of a scallion
24. . . . under ECOLOGY
28. Behold, biblical-style
29. "Xanadu" rock grp.
30. Synonym and anagram of "aye"
31. Toward the stern
34. Sch. requirement
35. Food product whose name was spelled out in old ads
38. Artist Picasso
40. Hip-hop
42. . . . under INTERIOR DECORATION
46. Hawaiian guitars, informally
48. Sch. requirement
49. Quaker pronoun
50. Change the decor of
51. Sink cloth
53. . . . under FASHION
55. ___ nous
56. Scornful expression
58. Houston baseballer
62. . . . under SOVIET FARMING
65. Walter of *The Odd Couple*
67. Be sore
70. Favoritism
71. Helen Reddy's "___ Woman"
72. Matching pieces
73. . . . under PSYCHOANALYSIS
78. Obtain
79. ___ profundo
80. Some PhD exams
81. Where Harrah's was founded
83. Lizzie Borden's weapon
84. Cul-de-___
87. Former RR regulator
88. Fan favorites
90. . . . under EDUCATION, PROBLEMS IN
95. Nod off
98. Austen title heroine
99. *La Dolce* ___
100. High wind?
101. Pilot's "back to you"
102. Help at a heist
103. Black, in poetry
104. Like lyrics
105. . . . under CHILD CARE
106. Fully cooked
107. Ply the needle
108. Prefix with stationary

DOWN

1. Cat call
2. Light brown hues
3. . . . under METEOROLOGY
4. Dress with the hem below the knees
5. Vessel that was once filled by dipping it by rope into a well
6. Cleared the throat
7. Models do it
8. Opposed
9. Theatrical
10. "Joy ___ World"
11. Lubricates
12. Stooge with a bowl-cut hairdo
13. Have debts
14. State tree of 19-Across
16. Irish actor Milo
17. Outlet for the Thames
25. This, to Juanita
26. Sacred
27. Snack with cerveza
31. Having what it takes
32. Took it on the lam
33. Dog that went to Oz
36. Limber
37. "With rings ___ fingers . . ."
39. Takes into custody
40. Ill-mannered
41. Of the same family
43. Star Trek series, for short
44. Sun. talk
45. Corp. VIP
47. Screeches
52. Sun. talker
53. Golfer's peg
54. Belfry undesirable
56. Cylindrical military cap
57. Polite refusal
59. . . . under ENTOMOLOGY
60. Miles per hour, e.g.
61. Give the heave-ho
63. Lawyers' org.
64. Actor Cage, informally
65. *SI* or *GQ*
66. Red-white-and-blue
67. Actress Jessica
68. Try to persuade
69. Hydrant attachment
71. Mark durably
74. Pear variety
75. Unsophisticated one
76. Nooks
77. Hester Prynne's stigma
82. Thou-shalt-nots
85. In the lead
86. Smallish band
89. River to Lyon
90. Transfusion fluids
91. Portent
92. Behind schedule
93. Load, as cargo
94. Brick maker
95. Opposite of doff
96. Eggs
97. Kind of Buddhism

FUTURE WORLD by Maura Jacobson

An eclectic set of puns on names from tomorrowland.

ACROSS

1 Garden pavilion
7 Explosion
12 Forge
18 Not ethically concerned
19 Way to go
20 Adjutant
21 President of the future?
23 Apportions out
24 Short-story writer Harte
25 Phiz
26 Ditties
28 Ballpoint, e.g.
29 Neckline type
32 Elvis's record label
33 Gallivant
36 Broadway song of the future?
42 ___ king
43 Political influence
44 Wine region of California
45 Whodunit award
47 Title role in a hit 1922 play
48 Old Roman household gods
51 Big ___ Conference
52 English novel of the future?
56 Paper quantity
58 Milk source
59 Some chest beaters
60 Sound from Simba
61 ___ Paulo, Brazil
64 Did a glissade
65 Parking monitors of the future?
69 "Be off!"
72 Chewy candy
74 The Coyote State: Abbr.
75 Snafu
77 Opposite of "writes in"
79 Certain sorority woman
80 Dick's running mate, twice
81 Traditional sitcom of the future?
85 Morning hour
86 The Matterhorn, e.g.
87 Foxy
88 "___ Miz"
89 Related on the mother's side
91 Berne's river
92 Piled up birthdays
96 Part of a foot
99 Oscar-winning actor/ director of the future?
104 Dracula and others
105 Nonsensical
106 Nobel-winning nun
107 Wrinkle
108 Lauder of cosmetics
109 Like the Dodge Charger and Porsche Boxster

DOWN

1 Attire
2 Love, to Ovid
3 Postal division
4 The "E" in QED
5 Parisian cotillion
6 "Grumpy" ones in a 1993 film
7 Boast
8 Myrna of the movies
9 Leo/Virgo mo.
10 Alphabet trio that's also a name
11 Camp sight
12 Luck
13 Paper signed before filming
14 Right-angle extensions
15 GI mail depot
16 Hanoi holiday
17 Places for gurneys, for short
22 Peewees
27 Ceramic piece
28 Peach discard
29 Caracas's land: Abbr.
30 ___-Car (rental company)
31 Violinist Mischa
33 Lady ___
34 "Poor, pitiful me!"
35 Pub missile
36 Dieter's possession
37 Macaroni shape
38 Cacophony
39 "Beauty and the Beast," e.g.
40 Pueblo Native Americans
41 Cereal bit
46 Blue Stater, for short
49 Slangy suffix with sock
50 Scorch the surface of
53 Comic-strip prince, for short
54 Homer's Iliad, for one
55 The scarlet letter
57 Escort's offering
60 Sublease
61 Secondary option for a DJ
62 "___ which will live in infamy": FDR
63 Werner or Schindler
64 Trifle
65 "Brood" animals
66 Cybercorrespondence
67 Irritable
68 Arthur of Wimbledon fame
69 Clobbered, old-style
70 Scouting outing
71 Yoked pair
73 Gun
76 Sun orbiters
78 Sun-related
79 Third word of "America"
82 Go by
83 Suitable
84 Flat hats
89 Europe's most active volcano
90 One of a noted quintet
91 To ___ (exactly)
92 Jackson 5 hairdo
93 Suffix with theater or opera
94 Once, formerly
95 WWII attack time
96 Former RR watchdog
97 Neither's partner
98 Take to court
100 Carry-___ (small luggage)
101 Diamond club
102 Afternoon hour
103 Money to put in an acct.

FOODIE FILM FESTIVAL by Elizabeth C. Gorski

It's not just popcorn at the movies now.

ACROSS

1 Sixth word of the "Battle Hymn of the Republic"
6 Sum
9 24-7 cash sources
13 ChapStick target
16 *Giant* actor Sal
17 Boisterous laugh
19 Actress Perlman
20 Volcanic fallout
21 Flick about a baseball farm team that knows its onions?
24 1051, on a landmark
25 Cinematographer Nykvist
26 Tear's partner
27 Milky gem
28 Cereal drama for which Angelina Jolie won an Oscar?
35 18-wheeler
36 Pageant accessory
37 The "I" of I. M. Pei
39 Not together
42 Classic film about pancake rage, with "The"?
48 Subway riders rail about them
50 "Catch ___ you can!"
51 Piglet's pal
52 Maven
53 Drill parts
54 "Flashdance" singer Cara
56 Psychological thriller about quahogs that won't come out of their shells, with "The"?
62 Rapper West
63 Tennis's Mandlikova
64 "Two hearts," e.g.
65 Suffix with cruciverbal
66 Expert
67 "Amen!"
73 Oscar-winning film about a Georgia beauty pursued by a royal?
77 See 12-Down
78 "Livin' La Vida ___"
79 Big name in coffeemakers
81 Burner setting
82 Film classic that serves up some Southern comfort?
88 Amazes
91 Possible nickname for Scrooge
92 Turn suddenly
93 Color
94 Comedy in which Meg Ryan finds love in a deli?
101 Suffix with Brooklyn
102 Rooftop revolver
103 Flight segment
104 Lush Hawaiian island
105 Microwave
106 Détente
107 Business card abbr.
108 Actor Edward James ___

DOWN

1 *Today* rival, for short
2 Pint-sized, in Dogpatch
3 Coffee order
4 Christopher of *Superman*
5 Sticks figure
6 "Woof"
7 Half an umlaut
8 "Well, lah-di-___!"
9 Pianist Claudio
10 Blackjack expert Edward O. ___
11 Kitty call
12 With 77-Across, Padres' home
13 Tiffany treasure
14 Española, e.g.
15 Punxsutawney prognosticator
18 Bandage over
22 Taking care of business
23 Suffix with bombard
27 Spray target
28 Tennis's Steffi
29 Kelly of morning TV
30 Make the cut?
31 Empty container weight
32 Mocedades hit "___ Tú"
33 Squabble
34 "Did I just step in . . . yuck!!"
38 Women's room in a palace
40 Answer
41 Musketeers' count
43 Give off
44 Funnyman Rogen
45 River to the Seine
46 A whole lot
47 Spade go-with
49 Cloud chamber particle
53 Creative person's deg.
54 Epic from Homer
55 Circle measurements
56 Pageant accessory
57 Blue-chip chip maker
58 Guzzle
59 Nature's pencil holders
60 "We're movin' ___!"
61 *Undercover Boss* network
62 This-and-that case
66 Wee biter
67 Tale
68 One ___ (kid's game)
69 "Nope!"
70 Frenzied excitement
71 "___ Rhythm"
72 Car trips that'll cost you
74 Keystone ___
75 Hosp. locale
76 Old Treasury offerings
80 St. Petersburg's river
83 R&B singer ___ Marie
84 "___ it!" ("My mistake!")
85 Modern, in Mannheim
86 *Wall Street* character Gordon, who said "Greed, for lack of a better word, is good"
87 Kidney-related
88 Phenom
89 Lead-in to sight
90 Cry
94 Grunt: Abbr.
95 "Go, team!"
96 Summer in Montréal
97 Ritter, the singing cowboy
98 Choose
99 ___ Paulo
100 Not hers

TIME LIMIT	YOUR TIME
30 MINUTES	

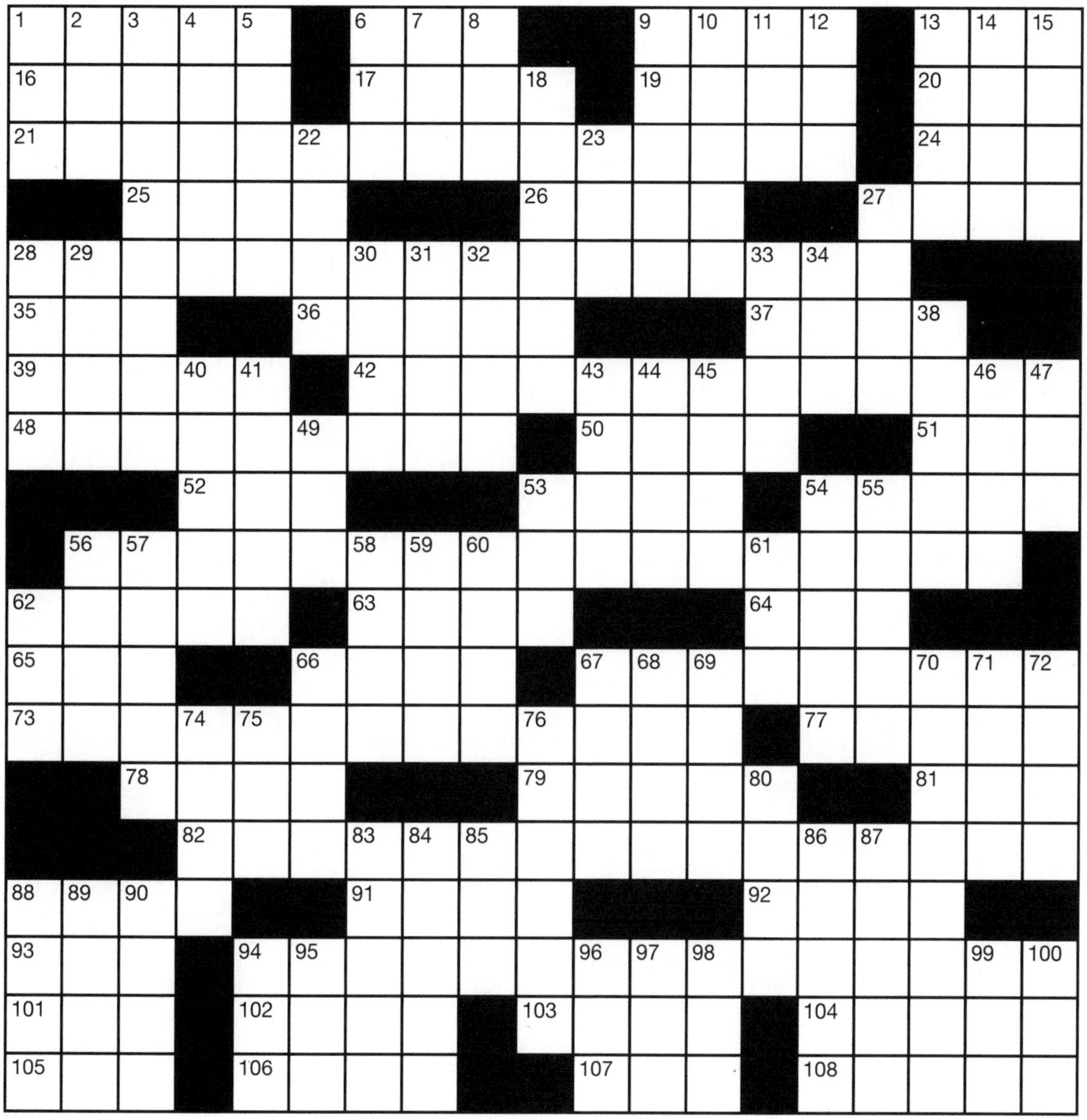

EVERYBODY LOVES A CLONE by Elizabeth C. Gorski

A puzzle that will have you seeing double.

ACROSS

1. "Lights out" music
5. Star Wars fighter
9. Western plateau
13. Octane Booster maker
16. It's the law
18. Ryan Seacrest's show, briefly
19. Make, as coffee
20. $$$ for old age
21. Wonderful chinaware contests?
24. Roar
25. Bobby-soxers, e.g.
26. Hoop grp.
27. Wearing stilettos, e.g.
29. Actress Mendes
30. Enter by oozing
32. Russia's ___ Mountains
33. Meddling with an Eastern princess?
38. Japanese sash
39. ___ Spiegel
40. Face cards?
41. Olympic skater Baiul
45. Stick-on
48. Maker of Glimmersticks eyeliner
50. U.F.O. occupants
51. Bagel go-with
52. Hollywood's Kazan
54. Freezer container
57. Kyrgyzstan's ___ Mountains
58. Kick in the rear?
61. End-of-semester events for nudists?
63. Swelled heads
64. Makes it big
66. Pinball no-no
67. Roman 555
68. Hot glue dispenser
69. Bellicose deity
71. Houses that have sitters?
74. Long battles
76. Misbehaving
78. Director Van Sant
80. Dig in, so to speak
81. The Addams Family character completely charms one small town?
86. One picking up speed?
88. Lifts
89. Bind
90. Give tacit approval to
92. Aunt, in Acapulco
93. Urban commuter's purchase
97. Doll
98. New York gallery's joint venture with Mrs. Smith?
101. Draw on
102. Stream
103. Fuss
104. Wipe clean
105. Tex-___ cuisine
106. Kitten's plaything
107. ___ arch
108. Lost traction

DOWN

1. Put through the paces
2. Together, musically
3. Organ part
4. Theater opening?
5. Triangular sails
6. Shogun's capital
7. Killjoy
8. "Don't worry about me"
9. Exec's degree, maybe
10. White fur
11. Spotted
12. "Heck, it was nothing"
13. The Beatles' "Hey Jude" vis-à-vis "Revolution"
14. Flutist's effect
15. Crummy reviews
17. Rome's ___ Fountain
22. ___ X
23. Stared with awe
28. "___ Tu" (1974 hit)
30. The "S" of 31-Down
31. Agcy. with auditors
33. 16 1/2 feet
34. "Honest" prez
35. "Way to go!"
36. Breakfast cupful
37. "In a minute . . ."
42. 1957 Alec Guinness film
43. Linguist Chomsky
44. Graph line
46. View on a Swiss postcard
47. Sass
49. Folk singer Phil
50. Often-pierced body part
53. Leo and Virgo's time
55. Ride up the slopes
56. Krypton or xenon
57. Bar in a car
58. Wine list section
59. Wrinkled citrus fruit
60. Partisan leader?
62. German article
65. Is absorbed by, as darkness
68. Settle in
70. Rodeo, e.g., in brief
72. Mark with graffiti
73. Canonized Fr. woman
75. Fortify
76. Cry in a manger
77. Curly-tailed dog
79. Stomach flattener
82. Mini-shake
83. Old salt
84. Smooth cotton fabric
85. Untouchables?
86. Alternative to a guillotine
87. Building addition
90. Bud
91. The Big Easy, for short
93. Org. with lodges
94. "Be ___"
95. Answer to a señor, maybe
96. Bye recipient
99. Grain bristle
100. Fruit drink

FAULTY KEYBOARD by Patrick Merrell

A puzzle with a lot of sticking points.

TIME LIMIT	YOUR TIME
25 MINUTES	

ACROSS

1 Go with the flow
5 "Little" boy in a children's book
10 They're put on for takeoffs
16 "Top" part?
17 Louse
18 One who's hard to get hold of
19 Cartoon gunfire sound
20 Charged
21 "Over my dead body!"
22 Big puffy cotton balls?
25 Chopin's "Nocturne ___ Major"
26 Deck clearer
27 Place for a pint
28 Posh
34 Holy Mlles.
37 Sound that might mean "I'm hungry!"
38 Mole
39 Keenness
41 Sitting Bull or Crazy Horse
44 Tolkien tree creature
45 Caesar salad bit
46 Amherst sch.
48 Dishware
49 Little-known facts
52 Post's opposite
53 Movie set light
57 Check box
58 Plumlike fruits
60 Dapper fellow
61 Quechua home
62 1960 #1 Elvis Presley hit . . . or an apt title for this puzzle
66 Farm college students, for short
68 Director Lee
69 Caustic soda
70 Change words?
78 Job applicant's mailing
79 Bird with an S-shaped neck
80 More than a couple
81 Twinkles
82 Pond scum
83 "Gimme ___"
84 Visit
85 Austin Powers portrayer
86 "Yo mama," e.g.

DOWN

1 Flagship New York station
2 Org. involved in the Scopes Monkey Trial
3 Haus wife
4 Silents cowboy star
5 Prepare for surgery
6 Asia's ___ Sea
7 It's what's for dinner
8 Texas oil port
9 Declines participation
10 Four-star off.
11 One-masted boat
12 Rare
13 "Seems unlikely"
14 Manage, as a bar
15 Some urban hotels, briefly
23 Burma's first prime minister
24 PC's "brain"
28 Notes before tis
29 Mentalist Geller
30 Common brainwashing site, it's said
31 Like Elmer Fudd's speech
32 McEwan and McKellen
33 Over-the-shoulder wrap
35 DDE's WWII command
36 Roget's offering: Abbr.
40 Pass (out)
42 Winners of the first World Cup, 1930
43 Comic book mutants
45 Spot for a chaw
47 Firm members: Abbr.
48 Swamp swimmer
49 Bonehead
50 Suffix with phon-
51 WWII Pacific battle locale
52 Having a mug like a horse
54 Answer with a raised hand
55 Lille liquid
56 Bearded grazer
58 Kitchen appliance brand
59 Salts in a foot bath, e.g.
63 ___ chi
64 Manhattan sch.
65 Meddlers
67 ___ cum laude
70 Energy units
71 Bombard
72 Remainder
73 Hankering
74 Char
75 ___ Minor
76 180's
77 Deerskin slip-ons

ALLOW ME TO INTRODUCE MYSELF
by Brendan Emmett Quigley

And if you didn't hear me the first time . . .

ACROSS

1 Supercilious reaction
6 Riffraff
11 Big tier?
16 Patisserie purchase
17 Call on a farm
18 "I don't give ___!"
19 It's full of rock bands
20 Jet alternative
21 Solvers' aids
22 Making a Taiwan city livable in the winter?
25 Scot's turndown
26 Director Anderson
27 Pennies: Abbr.
28 Monk's wine?
37 Informal approvals
38 Billet-doux closing
39 Toasty
40 Just one small bite
43 Bottle in a beach bag
45 A beer might be on it
46 Letter after Charlie
47 Bygone bulletin
48 Alternative to brick-and-mortar stores
50 With 82-Across, brayed
51 Menudo's kudos?
53 Annual Mummers Parade locale, informally
54 __ cosa (something else: Sp.)
56 "Yeah, right!"
57 Unwanted part of a bill
58 What the Arctic Circle is, population-wise?
63 P.D.A. number: Abbr.
64 Cyrano's nose
65 Fifth-century Chinese dynasty
67 Put some complete morons in touch with each other?
74 Hand-dyeing technique
75 Virginia's ___ Caverns
76 Tube with a prominent arch
77 Wonderland girl
78 "Give the dog ___"
79 Spirit of Russia?
80 Up
81 Dice game, informally
82 See 50-Across

DOWN

1 Disgrace
2 "All you do is criticize!"
3 Rubber
4 Rebuke to Brutus
5 Film vault holding
6 Goes back and forth on something?
7 Actor Giovanni of *Lost in Translation*
8 Ages and ages
9 Blab
10 Hall of Fame pitcher Waite ___
11 Papeete is its capital
12 Jerk in two directions
13 One of the Nereids
14 "Don't look at me"
15 Area 51's contents, purportedly
23 Came to
24 Sound of spring, for some
29 Sunrise direction
30 Did some above-average work
31 Salamander also known as the Mexican walking fish
32 Scribblings
33 Psalm ___, longest chapter in the Bible
34 Present at birth
35 Path
36 Suggest
40 Not standing
41 Enforcement strength, so to speak
42 Old Olds
43 One of 256 for Pac-Man
44 Leader who wrote *The Discovery of India*
47 Popular cologne
49 With 74-Down, place to get a tropical drink
52 Plunder
53 Bernard Madoff swindle, e.g., for short
55 "Behave!"
57 Stiff
59 Puzzle whose name means "cleverness squared"
60 In stock
61 Having gems arranged side by side, e.g.
62 Agree out of court
66 "Can't you hear me . . . ?!"
67 1988 LL Cool J hit "Going Back to ___"
68 Company whose business goes up and down?
69 Robed
70 Orchestra instrument
71 1982 film with a light cycle race
72 Small amount
73 Small amount
74 See 49-Down

33

CHANGE OF VENUE by Mike Shenk

Complete the word ladder to discover who is responsible.

ACROSS

1. Grab greedily, in slang
6. Prohibition
9. Professional runner
12. Typewriter key
15. Subject of a cry of "vive!"
16. Fit for red-carpet wear
18. *The Wire* carrier
19. Tiny amount to win by
20. *Second word in the ladder*
22. *Third word in the ladder*
24. Ancient coin worth a sixth of a drachma
25. Small pie
26. Ripe
28. Unable to pass the bar?
32. *Fourth word in the ladder*
35. Puts back to zero
36. *The Dick Van Dyke Show* family name
37. Group commanded by les générals
38. You may get a kick out of it
39. Spenser creations
43. *Fifth word in the ladder*
45. *Sixth word in the ladder*
47. Public houses
48. More pretentious
50. ___ Moore (canned stew brand)
51. Cathedral of Notre Dame locale
52. It might be withheld from a naughty child
53. *Seventh word in the ladder*
57. Less refined
58. Banks and Bushmiller
59. Roll of stamps
60. Star Wars princess
61. *Eighth word in the ladder*
68. *Ninth word in the ladder*
71. Lumberjacks' competition
72. Follower of many a dot
73. Stage name of U2 guitarist David Evans
74. Tennis star Dementieva

75. "Up, up, and away" advertiser
76. Baste
77. Address for the boss, maybe
78. Person responsible *[last word in the ladder]*

DOWN

1. Paving piece
2. Soft drink brand favored by Radar on *M*A*S*H*
3. Asia's ___ Sea
4. Muddy
5. Good place to start a word ladder
6. Ring setting?
7. Overhead
8. River spanned by the Peter the Great Bridge
9. Senate worker
10. Plastic ___ Band
11. Classic Ford
12. Place in which to nip a problem
13. Take in
14. *Charlie's Angels* assistant
17. European lang.
21. Act the loving grandparent
23. Stable particles
26. Sierra Club founder and family
27. Outstanding service
28. Bingham of *Baywatch*
29. It might have a frog in its throat
30. "What a piece of work ___!": Hamlet
31. Staggers
32. DVR button
33. Makes aquatints, e.g.
34. Cheerless
36. Cineaste's collectible
38. Minute groove
39. Fails to mention
40. France's patron saint

41. Words on a Wonderland cake
42. Better at artifice
44. Feet in a meter
46. Proportionate, as a duty
49. Reelection seekers
51. Sailor's reply
52. Set off, as an alarm
53. Exclusive
54. Afore this time
55. Riddle
56. It takes turns
57. Whirlybird
59. It's Welsh for "dwarf dog"
61. "What a relief!"
62. Big lug
63. Cones' counterparts
64. Concert highlight
65. Peak no.
66. Painter Magritte
67. Go through the roof
69. Roy Orbison's "___ Over"
70. Cow or sow

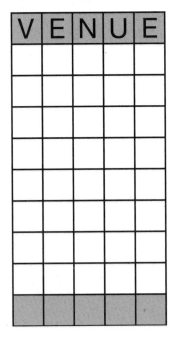

CAN WE TAWK? by Elizabeth C. Gorski

A puzzle that can be done in a New York minute . . . or 25.

ACROSS

1 Neither fem. nor neut.
5 Nails down, so to speak
9 Like some pools and arguments
15 1930s film "star" played by Skippy
16 Slugger in 1961 news
18 DC institution with a branch in Phila.
19 From ___ (baby step)
20 Grade sch. class
21 Takes the wrong way?
22 Untying the knot in Vegas?
25 Olympic marathoner Joan
26 Isle of ___ (Cambridgeshire locale)
27 Bread box?
30 It's good in Paris
31 Move, to a Realtor
33 Vampire
35 Group that performed "The Tears of a Clown"?
39 Not home
40 "All ___ consists in bringing something into existence": Aristotle
41 Feldman and Robbins
42 Racket
43 University instructor in origami?
47 Summer abroad
48 2009 film set in 2154
50 Show
51 Bankrupt
52 Have one's hair done by the salon apprentice?
57 Graff of *Mr. Belvedere*
58 "Why don't we?!"
59 Sister of Helios
60 Sugary ending
61 Part of a White House address
62 It often goes on the bottom
65 "No way!" . . . and a hint to 22-, 35-, 43- and 52-Across
70 Bargain-counter
73 *Spider-Man* director Sam
74 Water swirl
75 Universe
76 Prickly plant
77 Golden ___
78 Close-lipped
79 Title captain played by Charles Laughton
80 Talk of the Highlands

DOWN

1 One to whom a hat may be tipp'd
2 Take ___ at
3 Stir up
4 Jim Hawkins, e.g., in *Treasure Island*
5 Lennon classic
6 Diamond unit
7 La Salle of *ER*
8 In ___ (unmoved)
9 Musher's need
10 Renaissance patron
11 Green card co.
12 Aunt in Mexico City
13 Blowup at a copy shop: Abbr.
14 Sot's affliction, with "the"
17 Police officer's pride
23 Quiet place
24 Anticoagulant's target
27 Hobbyist
28 Blesser at Christmas dinner
29 Virginia of *Sideways*
31 Steak order
32 Tournament hopeful
33 Meal for a caterpillar
34 Condensed: Abbr.
35 Desk chair features
36 Everglades denizen
37 Talk, talk, talk
38 Patient form info, for short
39 Slowly
43 At serious risk of sunburn, say
44 It may come after you
45 Bakery window display
46 Educational basics, in brief
49 Not 43-Down, say
51 1965 #1 R&B hit for Fontella Bass
53 Sleep like ___
54 Recording studio echo
55 Auk or albatross
56 Casual Friday top
61 Popular word game
62 Brought under control
63 Bossy part?
64 "Trust the ___ touch" (slogan)
65 Fortune's partner
66 Versed in
67 Chocolate choice
68 503, at the Forum
69 Daly of TV's *Judging Amy*
70 IV measures
71 ___ polloi
72 Night sch. course

COUNTER OFFER by Pete Muller

Directions appear inside the puzzle.

ACROSS

1 Plug type
5 Homo erectus
11 *Gladiator* or *300*
15 Asian sea name
16 Language in which "thank you" is "dhanybhad"
17 "Hawaiian Wedding Song" accompaniment
18 *Pour ___* . . .
21 Part of a common Latin conjugation
22 Get ready in a hurry?
23 Cooperative people?
24 . . . *into a ___*
27 Follower of 49-Across
28 Actress Kunis of *Black Swan*
29 It might be carried by an entertainer
31 First name in Chicago politics
35 Winter stash, for some
38 *Fill to top with ___*
41 It is "deceptively simple and endlessly complicated," according to a famous practitioner
43 Sch. with the fight song "Anchors Aweigh"
44 Strain
45 *Mix vigorously, then add two tablespoons ___*
49 Common payday: Abbr.
50 Gang leader?
51 Singer Lovich
52 *Use a ___* . . .
55 Intimates
59 Doing
60 Sonny and Cher, and others
62 Prefix with phobia
63 Belg., Neth., and Lux. were part of it
66 . . . *to ___*
69 Favorite
73 Try
74 Landing site near Citi Field: Abbr.
75 *Enjoy your ___*
78 Beginning
79 It might have one or more sides
80 *A Treatise of Human Nature* author
81 Massage, in a way
82 Took in with amazement
83 Like Washington, Adams, or Madison: Abbr.

DOWN

1 Title of reverence overseas
2 Like words from the mouth of Jesus
3 Nickname for 1950s-'60s actress Gina
4 Short subject in a Christmas play?
5 Invalidate
6 Eat like a bird
7 World's second-largest city, behind Rome, 2,000 years ago
8 Bub
9 Gobs
10 Frasier's brother on *Frasier*
11 Indonesian island known for its coffee
12 Similar (to)
13 Moolah
14 Poses
19 Activity suffix
20 It might be recombinant
25 Slowly
26 Part of a pig
30 1950s bust
32 Location of the only WWII battle fought on US soil
33 Jalopy
34 Man of mystery
36 Notches on arrows
37 Single-masted sailboat
39 Photographer Adams
40 Western star
42 Large quantity
45 Wheat, for one
46 Touch
47 Baseball brothers
48 Mark up or down at a store
49 Word with swine or stomach
53 Erupts
54 Absent
56 Make bigger
57 A sailboat might be made with this
58 Anonymous people
61 Gangster Bugsy
64 "Ay-yi-yi!"
65 A-lister, e.g.
67 Stormed
68 Pendulum's path
69 One way to get to the top
70 Roughly
71 Word with ball or hall
72 Bit of force
76 Last in line
77 Baseball scoreboard letters

SHORT BREAKS by Mike Shenk

This one will take a little time.

ACROSS

1 Service man?
7 Marbles, so to speak
13 Prefix akin to equi-
16 *True Blood* waitress
17 Stable model
18 Short time added to two Across answers
19 Slightly better-than-average motorists?
21 Bringer of wisdom, some say
22 Cut (off)
23 Decisive step
24 Coy answer to "Will you?"
26 Words of approximation
28 Swindle, in slang
29 Empathize with
31 "Like that'll ever happen!"
33 Sighed word
34 Comment that's really cutting?
41 Passionate
42 More ticked off
43 Ending with depend or correspond
45 *Bullets Over Broadway* Oscar winner
46 Placed
47 He's won more acting Emmys than any other man
49 "As lightly her form bounded over the ___": Shelley
50 Frenetically busy
51 It turns litmus blue
52 Something passed that's too hot to handle?
56 Hypocritical talk
57 Pointer's word
58 Ready to be shot, perhaps
62 ___ jeans
63 Marco Polo's heading
67 Minimal
68 God of the underworld
71 Kitten coat
72 One of the Peróns
73 Advice for fearful rocket travelers?
76 Short time added to two Across answers
77 Provide with an improved view, perhaps
78 May Day baby, e.g.
79 Antlered animal
80 Catherine who owned a barn in Chicago
81 Is out

DOWN

1 Cellist Casals
2 Mail, e.g.
3 Minor mistakes
4 Top rating, at times
5 Encumbrance
6 Limit
7 Cash substitute
8 In need of irrigation
9 "When pigs fly!"
10 Ephemeral sculpting medium
11 Bestselling album of all time
12 Respectful reply
13 Pol's concern
14 Glimpse
15 ___ a customer
20 Go with the flow
25 Birth announcement beginning
27 Fertile spots
30 Like some 70-Downs
32 Dispatched
34 Short-lived
35 Shining example
36 Walt Whitman's "___ the Body Electric"
37 "___ I see you first!"
38 Singer/pianist Buddy
39 Kidney-based
40 Ring
41 Saddler's tool
44 Half of hex-
46 Health, to Henri
47 Jessica of *Sin City*
48 Diamond-shaped fish
50 Medieval musician
51 They're beyond belief
53 Pine
54 Conductor
55 Alamogordo's county
58 Bigger than big
59 Place for a piercing, perhaps
60 Limited support?
61 Salt's heading
62 Like some pockets
64 Previously, poetically
65 Rooster's cue
66 Lock
69 Capital symbol
70 Creature that may be 30-Down
74 Purpose
75 Pool tool

BOUSTROPHEDON by Patrick Merrell

adj. (and n.): having alternate lines running from left to right and right to left

ACROSS

1 Hounds' sounds
6 Cut marks
11 Split
16 *A Confederacy of Dunces* author
17 Set used for readings
18 Old-time ink color
19 A boustrophedon path of people often leads to it
22 Drink named for a stomach enzyme
23 Lots, e.g.
24 Old World tongue
26 Many a 99¢ purchase
28 Asset for a pitcher
29 Things gotten in history, e.g., for short
32 Crossed (out)
33 Rural boustrophedon chore
37 Pre-DVD combo
39 Negative conjunction
40 Kind of knife
41 Title in a Joel Chandler Harris title
44 Place
47 Tic ___
48 Somehow . . . and an alternative title for this puzzle
52 ___ bet (wagered correctly)
53 Stable performer in the '60s?
54 Yen
55 Scatter
57 Writer Fleming
59 Non-bid
63 Suburban boustrophedon chore
68 Sanctions
69 "So fancy-schmancy!"
70 "Phooey!"
71 Pro ___
72 TV's Dr. ___
73 Composer Georges
76 Stay with, in a bad way

78 Boustrophedon machines common in the '70s and '80s
84 Point starter, in many games
85 Town in a Hersey novel
86 Somewhat of a start?
87 Barely visible
88 Healthful food claim
89 Uses a set of keys

DOWN

1 Indeed
2 Widespread 20th-century disease victim
3 Bourbon monarch
4 Crew
5 Tramp
6 Homophone of 5-Down
7 Against
8 Affecting culture
9 Absorbed
10 *The Great Escape* setting
11 Sacrilege for a pastry chef
12 Line into NYC
13 Prefix with cycle
14 Stoked
15 Literary inits.
20 Group of courses
21 Downfall?
24 It starts in March in DC
25 Gun
27 Cushion addition
29 Game traditionally played on dirt
30 Candlelit locale, often
31 Place
33 Made pictures
34 Like some bobs
35 Tiler's figure
36 Lave
38 Worsted embroidery yarn
42 Cool, once
43 Uncontested advancement
45 Serpent's tail?
46 Record

48 QB's huddle-ending instruction, maybe
49 Singer Jones
50 Signed doc., e.g.
51 Shorten
52 See ___ threat
56 Online viewing
58 Small pest
60 Oblivion, metaphorically
61 Snowmobile part
62 Pine-___
64 Biblical verb
65 *The Cider House Rules* actress
66 Epitome of non-charisma
67 Luxury hotel chain
72 Easy mark
73 Foretoken
74 Spanish boy
75 Purpose of many a visit to a doctor
77 Cop car, to a dispatcher
78 Excellent, in rap slang
79 Origin of species?
80 Prefix with cycle
81 Places for sgts.
82 Bemoan
83 Geometrical figs.

AT ONE'S END'S WIT by Cathy Millhauser

Warning: Bad puns dead ahead!

ACROSS

1 Like a human flock
5 Outlined
11 Praise-penning poets
17 Role for Ingrid
18 Pension recipient
20 Trust
21 Store that carries foreign-made caskets?
23 By the deadline
24 Hebrew seconds
25 Letters about a landing
27 Lackey
28 Municipal chief
29 Gets measured for a casket?
34 Syllables after "peek"
35 Source of teen embarrassment, often
36 Final outcome
37 Start some ending words?
40 Ugly remark
44 Hawaii County seat
45 Bus. phone parts
47 It's west of Gt. Br.
48 Kind of registry
52 Where "That's all, Folks!" folks are interred?
56 Let accumulate
57 Film critic with the column "On the Town"
59 Morocco's capital
60 Theme from *The Departed*?
62 Dumbbells
63 It's quite a stretch
64 Digital displays: Abbr.
65 Drought ender
67 Scrooge's nephew
69 Gravedigger's association?
77 Avis pair
79 Online brokerage
80 ___ about (roughly)
81 Requirement for Paul Bunyan's last ride?
85 Banderillero targets
86 Kind of holiday
87 Hurdle for salmon
88 NBA Hall of Famer George
89 101-digit number
91 Prequel to *Six Feet Under*?
97 Garden-variety stars?
98 *Ms.* magazine founder
99 "Thunderation!"
100 Requisite
101 Three-volley salutes, say
102 *Curious George* authors H.A. and Margaret

DOWN

1 Ad ___
2 *Arabian Nights* woodcutter
3 Cry in a tot's game
4 Chas Addams piece
5 Speaker on the diamond
6 Band with the quadruple-platinum album *Out of Time*
7 Muscle contraction chem.
8 Half of a newsmaking 1955 merger
9 Mess up
10 Big manufacturer of scales
11 *The Mikado* costume part
12 "I hammered this here thumb!"
13 Chants
14 Small boat
15 Pesci's *My Cousin Vinny* costar
16 *Hägar the Horrible* pooch
19 "___ perpetua" (Idaho's motto)
22 60-min., as photo-lab service
26 Attached
28 Start to practice?
29 Come (from)
30 Florence flooder
31 Harden
32 *Wheel of Fortune* buy
33 Like some acids
35 TV's Donahue
38 Room in many a mortuary
39 Part of NB
41 State of oblivion
42 Name of eight popes
43 Some are eternal
46 Like some wills
48 Lawyer's filing
49 Grist for a certain mill
50 Cuckoo
51 Make a knight
52 Pensioner's age, in old Rome?
53 Miner matter . . .
54 . . . and its homophonic contraction . . .
55 . . . and another homophone
57 Pippi Longstocking, for one
58 Cushiness
61 Give a new label
62 Two-year-old's assertion
65 Hand-knotted rugs
66 Classroom worker
68 Hurt
70 Insect whose larvae feed on honeycombs
71 Hagen of *Reversal of Fortune*
72 Grade-school basics, initially
73 More eccentric
74 Close enough to shoot
75 When the sun is highest
76 Med. examiners, e.g.
78 "Doubly dead" Poe title girl
81 Generous donation
82 The rope of one's end?
83 Gush
84 Gushers
85 *Corpse Bride* director Burton
88 Popular candy in a bag
90 Dropped drug
92 Acronymic car of old
93 Card game cry
94 Card game cry
95 Puppet's backside?
96 NFL units

IF I WROTE THE DICTIONARY by Merl Reagle

Featuring 11 original deft-initions.

ACROSS

1 Raillike bird
5 Damage control, say
9 Copacetic
13 Hit TV show set in Las Vegas
16 Tip-top
17 Divided country
19 Cookie that predates crosswords
20 Snake in the grass
21 n. the act of tying shoestrings
23 Educator Horace
24 ". . . blessing ___ curse?"
25 Pianist Claudio
26 adj. pertaining to jazz singing
29 Puccini possessive
30 ___ out a win
33 Indicating no gas, as a gauge
34 Ostentatious
35 adj. obsessed with thinking that one can play the guitar
39 Google success
40 Enclosure to an ed.
41 Eight-hour shift
42 n. an all-male function; stag party
46 Most comfy
50 Intro to marketing?
51 Certain trucker's job
53 adj. marked by heavy blows, as a fight
56 Perfectly
58 Willing-to-work wanderer
59 Words of denial
60 n. muddy buildup on the soles of sneakers
61 IM sender
62 French phone greeting
63 Lee who sang the #1 hit "I'm Sorry"
65 n. capsules, tablets, etc.; drugstore stock
67 "Pull up a chair"
68 One of three cartoon ducks
69 Disparaged
71 adj. well-versed in the Scriptures
74 Sorento maker
75 Rombauer of cooking
79 Lee who directed *Brokeback Mountain*
80 n. the transforming of people into swine (see Circe)
84 Combination
88 13 qvadrvpled
89 English poet Hughes
90 Hostess ___ Balls
91 v. to inject with truth serum
94 Leading
96 DC summer clock setting
97 "Je t'___"
98 n. the practice of kissing in parked cars
101 See 6-Down
102 Normandy city
103 Scout unit
104 Asian nation suffix
105 Driveway sealer
106 Masseuse's target
107 Place on the schedule
108 Refine, as one's craft

DOWN

1 Deli meats
2 Musical "sweet potato"
3 Position again, as one's legs
4 Gone fishing, perhaps
5 Calypso cousin
6 With 101-Across, a crusty entreé
7 Pupil's place
8 Former liberal, briefly
9 "It's Impossible" singer
10 Paperless tests
11 Connoisseur of the grape
12 Wish in many a toast
13 Plastic-shoe brand
14 Fergie, formally
15 Piedmont country
18 "I could crush you like ___"
22 Sorry sort?
27 Plow pullers
28 "Must've been something ___"
31 Plant nuisance of the South
32 Modern missive
36 Modern music genre
37 Artist's asset
38 Cappuccino alternative
43 Maiden name intro
44 Old Roman dress
45 "Ain't Too Proud ___"
47 Frequently, in verse
48 Bygone gun
49 Lincoln's in-laws
52 Sported
53 Skewed view
54 Depart from the script
55 Sir Georg with a baton
57 "She's quite ___!"
58 "Wait a minute!"
60 Excite
61 Hearty brew
63 Sofia resident
64 Car maker's initials
65 Computer command
66 Steaming
68 Was reluctant to proceed
70 Maui music maker: Abbr.
72 Indonesian island
73 Houseplant spot
76 Reached, as the surface
77 Prince Rainier, for one
78 Pain reliever
81 Megacorporation
82 Bishops' hats
83 Early outcast
84 Good (at)
85 *Washington Post*, CNN, etc.
86 The thin picture
87 Pre-Xerox copy
92 Mardi Gras follower
93 EPA concern: Abbr.
95 Chop finely
99 Quintana ___ (Mexican state)
100 Decide

LIPSTICK ON A PIG by Merl Reagle

Seven puns that will make you snort.

ACROSS

1 Circulation boosters?
7 Physician-turned-rebel
10 O or W output: Abbr.
13 Online help, familiarly
17 Dalmatians, e.g.
18 Cookout cut
19 Airport shuttle, often
21 Skin softeners for pigs?
23 Vaudeville star of *Hellzapoppin'* fame
24 Au, Cu, or Pb
25 Covert comment
26 ___ Mae
27 Frown-line reducers for pigs?
31 ___ Bien Phu, Vietnam
32 "I'll take that as ___"
33 & 35 "Wild Thing" group, 1966
38 Breast enlargement for pigs?
44 Buenos ___
45 Plantation bundle
46 Commercial cost
47 Dispenser candy
48 Free of worry
50 End of a game
51 Convenient type of swinoplasty?
58 Get into a spot, say
59 Small streams
60 Step (up)
61 State south of Arizona
64 AK-47s and such
65 Steak selection
67 A necessary eight hours' worth for pigs?
71 It's below the tibia
72 One of us
73 Honey or sugar follower
74 Arias
75 Aromatic applications for pigs?
84 Baseball bird
85 Cold shower?
86 Japanese zither
88 What Cuba is part of
90 Pig's posttreatment query?
92 Wets
93 "___ reconsidered"
94 Eur-rupter?
95 Way back when
96 Fr. holy woman
97 "Is the adder better than the ___, / Because his painted skin contents the eye?": Shak.
98 Willie Mays catchphrase

DOWN

1 Hurt down deep
2 Rival of Reach
3 Ill-fated teen
4 Constance or Norma of the silents
5 From ___ Z
6 High-priced spreads
7 St. ___, Virgin Islands
8 Delhi tongue
9 Clampett portrayer
10 Sid's TV costar
11 Chip ingredient
12 Bouquet
13 Four-page sheet
14 Without being present, after "in"
15 Neighbor of Ont.
16 ID sought by phishers: Abbr.
20 Noodle ___
22 "The search ___"
28 Fixes
29 Fix
30 Exhausted
34 Memphis-to-Nashville dir.
35 Bugler's melody
36 Zilch, to Zola
37 Rice-shaped pasta
38 Beau for a doe
39 Kind of acid used in soap
40 Across-the-board
41 Anklebone
42 Purim's month
43 Sarah Palin boy
45 Pecking part
48 Nozzle setting
49 Diciembre follower
50 Shows curiosity
52 Words after bone or brush
53 Petite sweet
54 Worker probably not getting benefits
55 Son of Aphrodite
56 Brand of contact lens solution
57 ___ Saint Laurent
61 One with intelligence
62 Sweden's Palme
63 Woody Allen–like
65 Account
66 Half an old TV news duo
68 Sumptuous
69 Subtle skill
70 Good to go
71 Indian drums
74 Short agenda?
76 Present itself
77 Expensively edged
78 Antony and Cleopatra, e.g.
79 Actor Davis
80 Porter's "___ Paris"
81 Staircase support
82 Crown location
83 Mango's center
87 "All right, fine"
88 80-Down, to Caesar
89 Refusal in Rennes
91 "Let's make ___ true Daily Double"

THE SPORTS BAR by Patrick Berry

Where you can get the team spirit.

ACROSS

1 Increased by
5 Member of Jubal Early's army, informally
8 Not up or down
12 Web programmers use it
16 Venipuncture need
17 Wistful lament
19 Golden rule word
20 A large Mississippi tributary
21 Beer choice at The Sports Bar?
23 *South Park* boy
24 Actress Polo
25 Workshop owner with little help
26 Liquor choice at The Sports Bar?
29 Skin layer
31 Place to put a pot
32 Forest frolicker of myth
33 Peloponnesian War victor
35 Prepared big drinks at The Sports Bar?
39 Fruit center
40 Excessive
42 Org. that handles returns
43 Actress Gardner
44 Tailless beast
45 Not bubbly, as bubbly
46 Humorist Bombeck
49 Hubble of Hubble telescope fame
51 Next-to-last order of drinks at The Sports Bar?
55 Vacation spot
56 Charge
57 Physical makeup
58 CIA forerunner
60 Eton enrollees
63 Containers of cold beer on hot days at The Sports Bar?
69 Detached
71 Opposite of 1-Across
72 Barker of old films
73 Wahoo's home
74 Startling cry
75 Popcorn preparer's need
77 It won't show you everything
78 Tent securer
79 Unfortunate result when the taps go dry at The Sports Bar?
84 Marriageable
86 Emulate *The Thinker*, e.g.
87 Member of the baronage
88 Digs in the snow?
89 Choice of a smallish wine order at The Sports Bar?
93 Dogpatch boy
96 Repeated word in the name of the Kenneth Grahame character ___ of ___ Hall
97 Site of the Kit Carson House
98 Check too few IDs at The Sports Bar?
100 Quartet member
101 Salinger girl
102 Sierra Club founder John
103 Tourist city in Uttar Pradesh
104 Complain
105 Words in passing?
106 Start to buckle
107 Hardy girl

DOWN

1 College profs, often
2 Vega's constellation
3 "Out of bed, sleepyhead!"
4 Harder to hear
5 Shoot the breeze
6 "I Still See ___" (*Paint Your Wagon* song)
7 "The immortal god of harmony"
8 Lock horns
9 Mean
10 "Too many to list": Abbr.
11 Doomed
12 Setting for many a *Playboy* pictorial
13 1979 Peter Falk comedy
14 *The Tilled Field*, for one
15 Cut of meat
18 Illinois home to Rand McNally
22 Molière schemer
27 BO buys
28 Activist's raison d'être
30 More virile
33 Leisurely retreats
34 Half-___ (skateboarding site)
35 Constantly changing
36 Zoologist Fossey
37 Unholiness
38 Not mad
41 Brown or White
46 Iroquois foes
47 Massage vigorously
48 Dirty treatment?
50 Potluck contribution
52 "Assuming that's true . . ."
53 Film director Buñuel
54 Adding points to
59 Of the shoulder blade
60 Some of them are chocolate
61 Healing balm
62 Office name holder
64 French monthly
65 Language suffix
66 Activity for those who lack intelligence?
67 Spin
68 Wise
70 Impose (upon)
76 Uncarbonated beverage
77 Help for an insomniac
80 Completely lacking
81 Turn into
82 Doesn't just call
83 Hosp. locations
85 Bay lynx
88 *The Jewel in the Crown* setting
89 Knife
90 May Day centerpiece
91 Geared toward neophytes
92 Stigma
94 Misses the mark
95 Vitamin amts.
99 0.1 microjoule

HOOKED ON HOMOPHONICS by Merl Reagle

Or . . . "Thanks for Listening." An olio of aural puns.

ACROSS

1 Qualified
5 Twisted
11 James Garfield's middle name
16 Raised
17 Hynde of the Pretenders
19 Fruit with pink pulp
20 Good place to get a tummy tuck?
22 Pliny the ___
23 Grand slam in tennis?
24 Paulo or João
25 Gray area: Abbr.
27 Money that once came in denominations up to cinquecentomila
28 Comment at a Halloween party about an Oscar Mayer costume in the back of the room?
34 Petro-Canada competitor
35 Hole up
36 Cursor director
37 Parking place
40 Plus or minus
42 *The King and I* costar
43 Daily tally (seemingly) from inquisitive kids?
50 Misadd, e.g.
51 ". . . ___ combination thereof"
52 Rib
53 Words after "here" and "there," in a song
54 VW Rabbit?
57 Kate's "sneaky" brother?
60 Playground comeback
61 A void to avoid
65 Permissive
66 *Black Orpheus* setting
67 Constantly yelling fan . . . after a game?
72 Milan's Teatro ___ Scala
73 High-desert art colony
74 Friendly introduction?
75 Cattle-herding canine
77 End of an era?
79 Sushi bar soup
83 Remark regarding a barely profitable product?
89 Kind of wit
90 "___ Wood saw a saw saw wood as no other wood-saw Wood saw would saw wood" (old tongue-twister)
91 "Here ___ again"
92 Follow a pattern, maybe
93 Droid's "last name"
95 Collection of Hindu aphorisms on punctuation?
100 Manhattan, for one
101 Old enough to vote
102 Exfoliate
103 Bites the dust
104 Ups
105 It may carry a tune

DOWN

1 Related on the father's side
2 Big name in gift chocolate
3 Flood barriers
4 Female in a wool coat
5 Go by quickly and audibly
6 ___ antiqua (early European music)
7 Pants mishap
8 Omega preceder
9 Tavern sign abbr.
10 Jack's girl in a 1982 #1 hit
11 Jazz ___
12 1988 Kevin Costner film
13 Forearm bone
14 Opposed
15 Colt producer
17 Scorch
18 Where David slew Goliath
21 Ole Miss rival
26 Like tournament crosswords
29 Prankster's cry
30 Gomez Addams's pet name for his wife
31 Chowderhead
32 Smooth transition
33 Neighbor of Swe.
38 Alternatively, in chat rooms
39 Model/TV host Banks
41 "Chatter"-monitoring org.
42 Prepares to be knighted
43 Just-squeezed
44 Angelou's "Still ___"
45 Intro to "boom-de-ay"
46 Savanna slitherer
47 Romeo's love
48 ___ *with Love*
49 Not great, not awful
50 Utter, perhaps
55 "Could've been bad, but we're fine"
56 "This is only a test" org.
58 Some get caught on it
59 Prez, e.g.
62 "That being said . . ."
63 Language of South Africa
64 "Fudge!"
68 One of Chekhov's "three sisters"
69 As if they were twins
70 "Not from where ___"
71 Foe of Carthage
75 Foe of Caesar
76 Pain in the ear
78 Poetic regions
80 Conforming (with)
81 Car installation
82 Oldman's *JFK* role
84 Direction that becomes its own opposite by putting "o" in front
85 Old Indian title
86 "Hasta ___"
87 Actor Richard
88 Mil. bosses
89 Extra: Abbr.
94 Authorizations
96 Comic/activist Margaret
97 Tie-breaking periods: Abbr.
98 Intersected
99 Classic news inits.

LETTERHEADS by Patrick Berry

Wherein good things come in threes.

ACROSS

1 They have bell guards
6 Surface damage
11 Muffle
17 Rita Hayworth film featured in *The Shawshank Redemption*
18 Its state quarter depicts a peregrine falcon
19 Put notches in
20 Ode to satellite navigation?
22 Life-saving company?
23 Rarity on a crowded subway
24 Farmyard sound
25 Purse piece
27 Neighbor of Virgo
28 Clark's *Hee Haw* cohost
30 Midgard Serpent slayer
31 Take a bite of
33 Chevy Tahoe lights, e.g.?
36 Chinese restaurant chain that blocks solar radiation?
40 Where the heart is
41 Batter who famously followed Blake
44 Straight
45 Is obligated (to)
46 Coach who was *Sports Illustrated*'s 1993 Sportsman of the Year
47 Grandpa Munster's portrayer
48 Cuisine that uses fish sauce
49 Olympic sport until 1936
50 Bones in a macabre story
51 Resort facility
52 Story of Yogi's picnic basket find?
57 Kindergarten break
60 Summoned servants, say
61 *Commando* ___ (1950s sci-fi serial)
62 Not quite in the frame?
66 Oxford university
68 Pitcher's successes
69 Timeworn observation
70 Harridan
71 Retail clothing giant
72 Oscar winner for *Separate Tables*
73 Meal from an off-road drive-thru?
75 Television's Adrian Monk, to his therapist?
77 Put in
78 '10 or '11 person, say
80 Scandinavian love goddess
81 Anatomical duct
83 Ring bearer
84 Previously
85 Joel's seducer in *Risky Business*
89 Big part of a sci-fi film's budget?
92 Explosive weapons launched from bicycles?
95 Takes back
96 Host
97 Arkansas's ___ Mountains
98 Filtered
99 Guerrilla actions
100 Isn't rigid

DOWN

1 Bakery supply
2 Oil transporter
3 Lohengrin's bride
4 Post at the *Post*
5 *On the Road* narrator
6 Parlor furnishings
7 Possible solutions
8 Thumbs-down
9 Late riser?
10 Subequatorial part of the Pacific
11 Johnny of Hollywood
12 Go astray
13 Sound at a pound
14 Big Apple tabloid
15 Peut-___
16 *The Mysterious Island* character
19 Gobble
21 Follow directions
26 Viscous
29 Electrical unit
31 Grammy-winning Houston
32 Bank quote
33 Dundee dweller
34 "No way!"
35 Brightest star in Lyra
37 Sevigny of *Big Love*
38 Golf coach's concern
39 Winner of six Silver Slugger awards
41 Tommy of *That '70s Show*
42 Holiday song title starter
43 Indoor track runner
46 Goes across
47 Fast-food chain
50 Moisten
53 Female Irish patron saint
54 Mask-wearing film villain
55 Sole problem
56 Turn left, say?
57 Superstar
58 Came down
59 Seemingly everywhere
63 World's most populous island
64 A long time
65 Painter Magritte
67 Highway safety org.
68 Dishwashing need
69 Conan's late-night sidekick
71 Take shape
74 They're right at your fingertips
75 Bacchanals
76 Major suits?
79 Mell Lazarus strip
80 Illustrious
81 TV hookups
82 CIA exposé author Philip
83 Proved not to be colorfast
86 The first "A" in A. A. Milne
87 High-school outsider
88 Seeks info
90 Up-tempo jazz style
91 Ring Lardner's "Alibi ___"
93 Late first-century year
94 Break down

SAY WHAT? by Brendan Emmett Quigley

To start, it bears repeating . . .

ACROSS

1 Personal check?
8 Stretch a dollar
14 Washer or dryer: Abbr.
18 Leader of an ancient tribe
19 Where Mandarin Airlines is based
20 ___ Lee cakes
21 Party to a lawsuit regarding Japanese watches?
23 Pro side
24 Site of some ID theft
25 Coin worth 100 cents
26 "Ideas Worth Spreading" conference
27 Some comedy
29 French nobleman
30 Fighter for Dixie: Abbr.
32 Leopard's tail?
33 Stun
34 Big name in toothache relief
38 Cello in an Ozawa orchestra, e.g.?
42 Bubbly name
43 Policy expert
45 Filch
46 Utterly clueless
47 Vice President Stevenson
49 Fishermen, at times
51 *Live at ___* (1970 double-platinum album)
52 IV liquid that I'll pay for?
54 Old Testament book
56 POW site
57 With 76-Across, movie heroine who works at a textile factory
59 Constructs haphazardly
64 Slow
66 Jackets less likely to cause injury?
68 Start of a book series
72 Followed, as advice
74 They may have glass ceilings
75 Turning point in time
76 See 57-Across
77 They're split

79 Dining ___
80 What the *Wheel of Fortune* host wields at an auction?
83 Women's Media Center cofounder
85 And more
86 54°40', e.g.: Abbr.
87 American watcher, for short
89 Abbr. at the bottom of an application
90 Some films
92 Exchange rate overseer: Abbr.
94 Lessen plan?
96 Clarifying letters
99 Longtime Bee Gees record label
100 Beatles girl writing some notes?
104 Bearing
105 Deceived
106 "Lofty" one in a Thoreau poem
107 Old Testament book
108 Water whirls
109 Lowered

DOWN

1 Sight along una avenida
2 101-Down's partner
3 Overly formal
4 "And we'll ___ a cup o' kindness yet"
5 Refrain
6 Flipped out
7 Church closing
8 Alberta's Lac ___ Anne
9 "That's impossible"
10 The Matterhorn, e.g.
11 Nexus 10 competitor
12 One of a pair of door signs
13 Feels for
14 Abbr. on an order
15 Invigorating hike?
16 Used
17 *The Hangover* setting

22 Leader called a "traitor to his class," for short
28 Iconic thrash band with the debut album *Kill 'Em All*
29 Work on a car
31 Kalaallisut speaker
32 Juicer
34 Gather
35 Signal, in a way
36 *Twilight* heroine
37 It's a howler
39 Put away
40 *CSI* actress
41 Garmin display: Abbr.
44 Nursery observer
48 Stuck
50 Clipped
53 Lead-in for -centric
55 Muff
58 County seat in central California
60 Old-looking font
61 Clear wrap
62 Serviceable
63 Mass presentation
65 Measure of purity
67 Organic suffixes
68 When to recap scoring
69 *Ugly Betty* star
70 Celebrant
71 [Check back later]: Abbr.
73 Pro ___
78 Bell site
81 Big runaround
82 Decadent
84 Put away for good
88 Busyness
91 ___ *Lisa*
92 Put a name to a face, for short
93 L'heure du déjeuner
95 Used Gchat, e.g.
96 They may be put on at a black-tie party
97 Cap site
98 Kept in a barrel, say
101 2-Down's partner
102 CNBC subjs.
103 Subway stop: Abbr.

Ready to play

ACPT style

Done!

Round 3:
CHALLENGING

WILD KINGDOM by Bob Klahn

Or . . . Rev. Spooner goes to the zoo.

ACROSS

1 On
8 Lake source of the Mississippi
14 Absolute truth
20 Leathernecks
21 One may be superior
22 Get some air
23 Schoolboy's peaked headwear, once
24 Rodent mouthful?
26 Big cat
27 *Darling* ___ (Julie Andrews film)
28 Of the surrounding area
29 Jungle abodes
30 Hip New York City area
33 Swindler
34 Down-to-earth types?
35 Captain Ahab?
37 Torch bearer
41 Stays home?
43 Word before drum or trumpet
44 Bit of broccoli
46 Figure of speech
48 Lepidoptera?
52 They're nuts
54 Play one's last card
55 Deviation in a ship's course
56 No for an answer
57 Father
58 Met expectations?
60 Out-and-out successes in baseball?: Abbr.
62 Pastoral composition
64 Cootie hell?
68 Deep gulf
71 Lawyer: Abbr.
72 They've been seen before
73 Taj Mahal site
77 ___ good turn
78 Emergency PC key
80 Fathers
81 Ventilate
83 Fragment of an SOS from a *Jaws* victim?
87 Weeper of myth
88 All the rage
89 Architect who graduated from MIT
90 Wheedles
93 Peak piled on Pelion
94 "Dam it!"?
98 It makes fat fast
101 Core group
104 Philosopher Thomas
105 Charles barker
106 *Boston Legal* star
109 Exercises
110 Chalkiness
112 What briar patches may be doing?
116 Spectacular procession
117 *Twelfth Night* countess
118 Duo
119 Royal staff
120 Gift getters
121 Gretel's brother
122 Sputtered cry

DOWN

1 Don of *Cocoon*
2 Skipped, as a dance
3 Exclusive fish story?
4 Quoits
5 Sun-worshipping empire
6 Insufficiencies
7 Medium strength?
8 Lift one's spirits?
9 Privy
10 Upstate New York prison
11 ___-devil
12 Head honcho
13 Chow line?
14 US naval base in Cuba, informally
15 Where to see *The Sopranos*
16 Abu Dhabi, for one
17 Prune
18 Razzmatazz
19 Estonian's neighbor
25 Jamie of *M*A*S*H*
27 Tripping tune
31 Charlotte of *Diff'rent Strokes*
32 Salary negotiator
33 *What's My Line?* punster
35 Tiny triller
36 DC auditors
38 Double-edged humor
39 Ore core
40 Leaded gas
42 ___ Book Club
44 Mtge. market stabilizer
45 Clark's partner in exploring
46 Beer barrel poker?
47 Label that signed Elvis
48 Barbizon School artist
49 Shirk work
50 The Inn is here
51 Cicely of *Roots*
53 Plot thickener
54 Adventure
59 Light pinkish yellow
60 Bo of *10*
61 +
63 Sugar
65 Edit
66 Münster mister
67 "Made in ___"
68 Beef up
69 Vulgarians
70 *Breaking Away* director Peter
74 Barnyard fowl party ticket?
75 Massage
76 Took some courses
79 Mudhole
80 Hindu destroyer
82 "Need You Tonight" group
84 Quiescent
85 Olympic sword
86 Aegean or Adriatic
90 Snookers
91 Boy-girl connection
92 You won't find it in *Consumer Reports*
94 Chilly reaction
95 Outfits
96 Take stock?
97 *Night* memoirist
99 Pothead
100 Playwright who declined the 1964 Nobel Prize
102 "Tomorrow" girl
103 *L'Absinthe* artist
105 Hebrew leader?
106 Like racehorses' feet
107 Hawaiian port
108 Possible score after 40-40
111 Writer James
113 Hamburger beef
114 Flapper wrapper
115 Chignon
116 Letter extensions: Abbr.

WHERE OH WHERE? by Oliver Hill

The directions could not be simpler.

ACROSS

1 Perfect husband material
8 1969 Dustin Hoffman role
13 Actor Lyle of TV and film
19 The merchant in *The Merchant of Venice*
20 Standards of perfection
22 Actor Estevez
23 Crushes
24 Some employee coverage
25 Car available in black . . . or black
26 Leave, as on a journey
27 Gym teacher's order
29 The South of Spain
30 Stuff
32 Get an ___ (ace)
33 Past, present, or future
35 Play direction
42 Séance sound
45 Nervous
48 "___, vidi, vici"
49 Pundit
50 Explanation with "Because"
53 Pungent sauce
55 Yalies
56 Got together
57 Routine material
58 Abandon
60 Hebrew name meaning "My God is God"
61 Transition
62 Comics cat
65 Stuck and bad off
72 Make a big do?
73 Letter-shaped bar
74 Slangy goodbyes
75 Maiden
79 Not at all subtle
80 John of TV's *Full House*
81 "___ deal!"
82 Wagon train locale
85 Antiabortion
86 Unpopular sorts
88 Fervor
89 Bizarre
91 *Illmatic* rapper
92 Leaders of exemplary lives
94 Prefix with frost
97 "Just ___ suspected!"
98 Some mild cheeses
101 Site of a Santa Ana victory
105 Abandoned and in peril
112 "Eat fresh" or "Just do it"
113 Cry "uncle!"
114 Former San Francisco mayor Joseph
115 TV's ___ *Girls*
116 God of the universe in ancient Egypt
117 Nauseate
118 Home of Tahiti and Samoa
119 Joe of the Three Stooges
120 Plowmaker John
121 The way water flows

DOWN

1 En ___
2 Semiconductor giant
3 Editors' marks
4 Peak before falling
5 Guarantee
6 Very funny person
7 "Sweet!"
8 Mountain line
9 Revoke, as a legacy
10 Camping equipment
11 Took a chair
12 *Lemony Snicket* villain
13 Andante and larghetto
14 Invoice figures
15 Tops of cans
16 "Yuck!"
17 Get greased, as a weightlifter
18 Kiddies
21 ___-mo
28 Two to one, e.g.
30 "That ___ excuse!"
31 Vietnamese New Year
34 Wall St. initialism
35 Gabor and Longoria
36 Marks (out)
37 Relative of Ltd.
38 Wows
39 Storm wind
40 Mideast bigwig
41 Extreme liberal
42 Rebel
43 Sanctuaries
44 Cause of a stock market sell-off
46 Cheap smoke
47 Turkic Russian
51 Pastry chef, at times
52 Use a backspace key on
54 Honey's place
57 Israelites
58 Party preparation
59 Precise: Sp.
61 Reggae precursor
62 Strong, to Jorge
63 Coup d'___
64 Flight
66 Electric ___
67 More than portly
68 Gauge part
69 Confine, as lake water
70 Bath sponge
71 Some test track turns
75 Unearth
76 Had a healthy diet
77 Blink of an eye: Abbr.
78 H. H. Munro's pen name
79 Hooters
80 Mob follower?
82 Half of an old TV couple
83 Side away from the wind
84 Vice President Quayle
85 Southpaws' opposites
87 Height
90 Abbr. after 45
93 1987 box office flop
95 Croquet need
96 Baseball great Roberto
98 Elicit
99 Check
100 In unison
102 In the past, old-style
103 *West Side Story* girl
104 When *SNL* ends
105 Word processor setting
106 Celebrity
107 Uncovers, poetically
108 Reagan and others
109 Existed
110 Foul-smelling
111 Nasty infestation
112 Sets (on)
115 Set, as the sun

ADDITIONAL CAST by Mike Shenk

Everyone wants to get into the act.

ACROSS

1 Common visitor's gift
8 Its capital is N'Djamena
12 Sketch holder
15 Fold female
18 Left
20 Printer's line
21 It might make a deposit
22 Lush tract
23 Comedy with Idle as a year-round Yankee?
27 Where some vets fought
28 Sails' staffs
29 Low-budget remake of *Planet of the Apes* starring Farrow?
30 Like a new dollar bill
33 Swagger
35 Soil aerators
36 Big atlas section
37 When les étoiles twinkle
39 Kingston Trio hit of 1959
40 Binoculars part
41 Film with Hunter as an agent denying iffy insurance claims?
51 Inauguration Day highlight
52 River through Orléans
53 Comedian Boosler
54 BBQ item
57 Genealogy chart
58 Prunes
59 Harmony
60 Candle count
61 Plenty
63 Playwright Pirandello
64 Enter a password, perhaps
66 Screwball comedy with Chappelle as a careless med school student?
72 Pop
73 Volcano features
74 Speaker's name
75 Cleaning aid
76 Jam and butter
79 Kind of market
81 Org. whose motto is "Maintiens le droit"
85 Brewpub brew
86 *The Devil's Dictionary* author
87 Soapy minerals
88 Head locks
89 Biopic about George Clinton's R&B group with Neeson?
92 Can't-remember-the-lyrics bit

95 Flamenco cry
96 Washday unit
97 Take ___ the chin
98 Shaker formula
102 Screen speck
105 Object on the cover of Pink Floyd's *The Dark Side of the Moon*
108 Comedy with Derek as a roguish pooch?
111 Camp David Accords signer
113 The Indigo Girls, e.g.
114 Sci-fi film with Henie fighting mutant organisms from bad preserves?
118 River to the North Sea
119 Big busyness
120 Alec's TV costar
121 Acts the peacemaker
122 Boston Garden legend
123 Go from side to side
124 Go from side to side
125 What's the holdup?

DOWN

1 Currency of 8-Across
2 Truman's birthplace
3 "I'll be right with you"
4 Field for Ares
5 One of the Manning brothers
6 Birds in Scheherazade's tales
7 Center actions
8 Rail connection
9 See 56-Down
10 "Sorry to say . . ."
11 Sister of Nora Ephron
12 Advance
13 Departments
14 Official with a list
15 Precocious Plaza resident
16 Crossed the threshold
17 Unchallenging classes
19 Chew (on)
24 Group behind the Constitution
25 K-O connector
26 Like beaver tails
31 Article dividers
32 Clingstone stone
34 Chinese dynasty during Christ's time
38 Old candle material
41 Cartographer's town

42 Crew member
43 Diner seating choice
44 Impudence
45 Casual pants
46 Somber stanzas
47 Wildly energetic
48 "Science Guy" Bill
49 Powerful bunch
50 Magnetic flux density units
54 Blow up
55 Noted lab assistant
56 With 9-Down, 1880 bestseller
59 Gives the boot
62 Doesn't bother
63 One with a mortgage
65 Catch, in a way
66 Citizenship type
67 Yen
68 Turn outward
69 Get in touch with
70 Primitive calculators
71 Like the familiar shark fin
72 It offers support
77 Chart shape
78 No longer active, in the mil.
79 Pre-practice ordeal
80 Architectural extension
82 Seat seeker
83 Caltech rival
84 Twosomes: Abbr.
87 Charm
89 Spiritual nourishment
90 Grammy category
91 Barbershop challenge
92 Lusty drive
93 Penitent person
94 Shutter feature
98 "___ hand?"
99 Tell tale item
100 Stereo inserts
101 Spacious apartments
103 Wax-wrapped product
104 Surgical tool
106 Less hesitant
107 Antiquated
109 *Saving Private Ryan* setting
110 Purchase
112 List title
115 Words with dime or diet
116 Fountain pen part
117 Bout bit

HEADS OF STATE by Merl Reagle

What a difference a couple of letters make.

ACROSS

1 Centers for dissenters
7 Beethoven's "___ Solemnis"
12 Quick tempo
20 Slow tempo
21 Like some buckets or barrels
22 Science museum exhibits
23 Origami?
25 Craft fair folks
26 Some Chicago trains
27 He played a cat with no backbone
28 Snitched
30 "Fancy ___"
31 Whacked, old-style
33 Like some political scandals?
39 "Good ___!"
42 Director Kazan
43 Overcooks
44 Tool in *The Shining*
45 British college entrance exams
49 Harried bus. owner's need
51 Many a state name in DC
52 Oversupply
53 Advice to a cougher?
55 Gutter site
57 Siphon off, as support
58 What a graph may illustrate
59 Number of players on *La Ruota Della Fortuna*
60 Eatery at an oasis?
62 You stay here
63 Iffy stat in a storm: Abbr.
64 Peeved
65 Steady the arrow
66 Film about boastful jerks?
75 Chevron's business
76 Doing mess prep
77 Apply
78 Pizarro's prize
79 Antoinette after hearing her fate?
84 Ended up with
85 Buddy on TV
87 Lots (of)
88 Adams and Grant
89 Answer to "What do you want on your BLT, Rocky?"
91 Nascar's Yarborough
92 Gen.-turned-pres.
93 And things of that ilk: Abbr.
95 Rascality
96 "Facts ___ facts"

97 Good, to Garcia
99 Speed Wagons, e.g.
101 Author Auletta
102 How you can tell where the candle was?
106 Face care brand
110 Escape route city, in *Casablanca*
111 Just right
112 Missay, as lines
115 Drink on draught
116 "Heaven forbid!"
120 "Jumble" solvin' dude?
123 Requires more than one, as to tango
124 Try a get-hitched-quick scheme
125 Stand up for (oneself)
126 Wises (up)
127 Vacations
128 Big ___ (the drug industry)

DOWN

1 Looks awed
2 Mo or Stew of Arizona
3 Oversight
4 Census datum
5 "You go, ___!"
6 Tough item to get up stairs, typically
7 *Tuesdays with ___*
8 Last words of *Who's Afraid of Virginia Woolf?*
9 Jumpy
10 Ladies of Lima
11 Go fishing
12 "___ approved"
13 Flying
14 "Hah!"
15 Olympic hurdles?
16 Some bow ties
17 Org. that does patient work
18 Pink-slip
19 Count addition?
24 Physicist Georg
29 Award for Sgt. York: Abbr.
32 Interlaced
34 Candidate list
35 Shower's partner
36 Limb gripper
37 Ooze out
38 Thwart
40 In-crowd outsider

41 Creepy cinema street
45 When Otello dies
46 Fictional Doone
47 "___ can do it"
48 ___ voce
50 Rip to bits
52 Pine-Sol target
54 Language that gave us "thug"
56 Iowa college town
57 Clean up your language?
60 Singer Sam
61 RSVP enclosure
63 Palindromic magazine title
64 *CSI: NY* star
67 Sue Grafton's "N"
68 Essence
69 *Motel Hell* star Calhoun
70 Floater for boaters
71 Tycoon on the Titanic
72 Whoopi's predecessor on *The View*
73 Gloomy, to poets
74 One of the Corleones
79 Cousin of the cockatoo
80 Leigh's 1939 Oscar role
81 Cartier competitor
82 Revealed
83 Church chorus
84 Dance related to a horse's gait
85 Brink
86 Magli of shoe fame
89 They know the score
90 Fine and dandy
92 "Ha-cha-cha-chaaaaaaa!" crier
94 Syrupy stuff
97 Absolutely minimal
98 Giant who wore #4
100 French verb with "nous"
103 Sulking sort
104 Canadian chowderhead
105 "Hot" place to chill
107 Debussy work
108 Great perturbation
109 Tale spreader
113 Dust-up
114 Creel contents
116 "___ official . . ."
117 Show-off
118 Volga tributary
119 Lean-___
121 Fitting
122 Intel processor?: Abbr.

KANGAROO PHRASES by Ashish Vengsarkar and Narayan Venkatasubramanyan

In which eight answers are elegantly self-defined.

ACROSS

1 Language maven Zimmer
4 Plato's portico
8 Big bill, slangily
13 "Brrr!"
19 Tow trucks
21 "Hot diggity!"
22 Deep disgust
23 [See highlighted letters]
25 Sewer line?
26 Dr. ___
27 Webster's shelfmate
28 Writers' righters
29 [See highlighted letters]
34 1950s South Korean leader
35 ___ soda
36 Louis, par exemple
37 Sino-Portuguese peninsula
41 1950s political inits.
42 [See highlighted letters]
48 It's measured in litres
50 College in New Rochelle, NY
51 Letters meaning "Read this"
52 US 1, e.g.: Abbr.
53 Attention getter
55 Beatle follower?
57 Jolt, for one
60 [See highlighted letters]
66 Spanking
69 Co-czar of Peter I
70 Number of signers of the Declaration of Independence, in Roman numerals
71 Vietnamese neighbor
72 "Veni," translated
73 Tony winner Patrick
74 [See highlighted letters]
79 The Police, e.g.
81 Sister of Clio
82 French silk
83 Pitchfork-shaped letter
85 Randomizer
88 First name in gorilla research
89 Sinew
93 [See highlighted letters]
99 1950s political nickname
100 Grab the tab
101 Wide, as a wingtip
102 Cash extender?

103 Sci-fi princess
104 [See highlighted letters]
111 "Be brave"
114 Zoroastrian in Mumbai
115 Uris protagonist
116 Mexican American, e.g.
117 [See highlighted letters, summarizing this puzzle's theme]
122 Calls up
123 Catty
124 Priest, not a beast
125 Leave
126 Choreographer de Mille
127 Mercury and Mars
128 Series ender: Abbr.

DOWN

1 DC-area arrival point
2 Slight stumbles
3 Least cool
4 Kind of shooting
5 Hill in Haifa
6 ". . . ___ quit!"
7 Generally speaking
8 Stuff
9 Penguin or Duck
10 Posthumous profiles
11 Shaven crown
12 Vision
13 Prefix with mural
14 "Great soul"
15 Vituperate
16 Hosea, in the Douay Bible
17 A Book of Nonsense writer
18 Pops
20 Bistro handout
24 One of the Cyclades
28 Instruct morally
29 Kind of shooting
30 Thrilling cry
31 Big Sur retreat
32 Singer
33 Disappearance sound effect
38 Mai tai liqueur
39 Craft
40 French article
42 "Me, too"
43 Porous iron ore
44 Cartful

45 ___ time (quickly)
46 Follow
47 [as written]
49 Comic Gilda
54 On Liberty writer
56 Here no more
58 Hamlet Oscar winner
59 Rootless vegetation
60 Newsman Lehrer
61 Some spawn
62 Honky-tonk
63 Gardner of Mogambo
64 "Feels so-o-o good!"
65 Goes bad
67 Metric measures: Abbr.
68 OED entry with 430+ senses
75 "Ring Cycle" goddess
76 Depilatory brand
77 "Let's leave ___ that"
78 Until the due date
80 Prefix with meter
83 Winter Seattle hrs.
84 Cry before and after "no"
86 Klutzy
87 German donkey
90 Requiem hymn
91 Any Joad
92 Nigh
94 Goulash flavorer
95 Ten in the looks department
96 Summoning, in a way
97 Words said with a pat on the head
98 "Gloria in excelsis ___"
103 Space systems maker
105 Perch
106 ___ to go
107 ___ Triomphe
108 Man and Skye
109 Born, in Brittany
110 St. ___ (London site)
111 Left in a hurry
112 Overhang
113 On
117 Lee's org.
118 ___-Cat
119 Mathematician's "ta-da!"
120 Defib expert
121 Pericardium, for one

AT LAST! by Mike Shenk

A Sunday-size crossword with a little something added.

ACROSS

1 City in the shadow of Mt. Rainier
7 Takes on
14 Copy room bundles
19 Unconcerned with right and wrong
20 How pie may be served
21 Lose one's temper with
22 Superhero abilities destined to prove victorious?
24 Burning
25 Hot temper
26 Peninsula with a DMZ: Abbr.
27 When Schweine fly
28 Lynx between lions?
30 Stereotypical mathletes
32 Takes in, say
35 PC on a network
36 Six-pack components
37 Whirlpool line
39 Foremost
41 Airport code that better not describe the security there
42 The 1905 Runabout, for one
43 Question to a delusional butcher?
49 Jazz legend Kenton
50 Missing
51 Mauna ___
52 PD broadcast
53 Program carrier
55 Acted the advocate
56 Curare carrier
57 Consult for help
59 Round number?
60 Unit now called a siemens
62 "Stay clear of the tusks when spearing," say?
68 Paper units
71 Silents star Murray
72 Ability to meet obligations
73 Hippodrome?
76 Born, in Bordeaux
77 Bar fixture
78 Stringency, in Stratford
79 Point out
81 *Lone Wolf* writer Picoult
82 Sari, e.g.
84 Nickname
86 1989 Broadway monodrama
87 Final answer in *Slumdog Millionaire*
89 Honey bunch
90 Fight between baby sharks?
93 CIO's partner
94 Blackhawks' home, in slang
96 One in a bireme bank
97 Mumbai master
98 You, to Johann
99 "Listen!"
101 Like refueling from a Stratotanker
104 Makes quieter
108 Flying a sleigh or fitting down a narrow chimney?
111 Foe of Dems.
112 Austrian article
114 Bulldog backer
115 Focused
116 Getting into a Volkswagen?
120 Play list
121 Yalta setting
122 Arboreal lizard
123 Victoria's Secret buy
124 2005 hit for 3 Doors Down
125 Bleep

DOWN

1 Trivial putt
2 Subject of many arias
3 Betray fear
4 Smelter supply
5 Sharpshooter
6 Not to mention
7 Satisfied sound
8 Point of view
9 Debussy contemporary
10 Author Eco
11 A Stooge
12 Mellow cheese
13 Became prevalent
14 One might be a real jerk
15 *Vogue* competitor
16 Separately priced
17 Sleeper with a soft bed
18 Western topper
21 When tripled, "and so on"
23 Sedative, slangily
29 Bonehead
31 Obsolescent
33 Boxer Ali
34 Body of an organism
38 Feet above sea level: Abbr.
40 Tummy ache soother
43 Noisy pup
44 First half of a Beatles title
45 Email address, often
46 Standard
47 Floor covering in a teahouse
48 Touches
49 Rude push
53 "I've had enough!"
54 Barrel piece
56 Singer born in Kaka'ako
58 River through Lake Geneva
60 Skimpy skirts
61 1890s Texas governor Jim and family
63 47-Down, for one
64 Treating cruelly
65 Seal up, in a way
66 Region of eastern Canada
67 Key worker?
69 Car quartet
70 Riyadh resident
74 Mockumentary after *Borat*
75 Opponent for un matador
80 Rwandan people
81 ___ Juice (smoothies chain)
82 Rebellious act
83 Let up
85 Ceiling support
87 Stuttgart sigh
88 Bodybuilder's hostility, maybe
89 Paul McCartney, e.g.
90 Pink-slip
91 Three-letter chunk
92 Guitar's first sound
94 1923 portrayer of Quasimodo
95 Axe handles
100 Afghan capital
102 English writer Smith
103 Impressionist work?
105 Some Southwest terrain
106 City north of Dallas
107 Pear-shaped instrument
109 Watch over
110 Illegal hit
113 Many a John Ford film
117 "But is it ___?"
118 Prefix with colonial
119 Symbol on the Argentine flag

THE LONG AND THE SHORT OF IT by Patrick Berry

Pronunciation is being butchered, and vowel play is suspected.

ACROSS

1 Key Watergate witness
5 Bubbling over
10 World's most populous island
14 It's used for walkie-talkie transmissions
17 Card's stock
19 Knight's weapon
20 Big production
21 Academic ordeal
22 Nibbles while others are praying?
25 Roman orator
26 Bit of advice
27 Old man
28 Pod-bearing plant
29 Rudolph's master
30 Hypoallergenic fleece sources
34 Men's garment made of lathing?
37 What the Second Amendment gives one the right to do
39 Have beefs, say
40 ___ Pieces
41 Video camera button
42 Picture of a mountain decorating a bank draft?
47 Soprano's repertoire
49 Barrett of Pink Floyd
50 Character of a people
51 Savory sauce
54 Man caves
55 "I'd almost forgotten"
58 Spiteful laugh
59 Harden (to)
61 More out there, as humor
63 Auto company named after the Pleiades star cluster
65 Ideas that spread virally
66 Visible items in the painting *Winslet Standing Fearfully on Chair*?
71 Charred
73 Relieves
74 Houston nine
77 Get together
78 Certain cage component
79 April occurrence
83 Make out
84 Ready to hit the roof
85 Trig ratios
87 Buddyroo
88 Rouse
89 Watch lousy TV shows?
94 Game akin to crazy eights
95 Work on in the editing room
98 Barley alternative, in brewing
99 Showing some growth
101 Water dogs, collectively?
106 Lovingly embraces
107 De-squeaked
108 ___ de vivre
109 Neb. neighbor
111 Corp. honcho
112 Redford's *Havana* costar
113 Make a sweater softer?
119 P.M. under George III
120 Twice quadri-
121 Plow man
122 Delicate headpiece
123 Bathing facility
124 Berkshire institution
125 Crime often linked to fraud
126 Quaint exclamation

DOWN

1 They play at work
2 Unimaginable time
3 Blotter abbr.
4 Bud drinker's quaff?
5 "Prince ___" (*Aladdin* song)
6 They play at work
7 At hand if needed
8 Prince of Wales's motto
9 General of the South
10 Other bad drivers, so to speak
11 Separately
12 Anglican clergyman
13 Untouched service
14 Titania and Oberon circle it
15 Oscar winner McDaniel
16 Vehicles that typically travel at 2–3 miles per hour
18 Tops of a mountain?
21 Ric of the Cars
23 Successful second ball
24 *Faust* writer
29 Blueprint detail
30 Scrape
31 Looked like a wolf
32 Fidgety alumnus?
33 Bomb's opposite
35 DC baseballer
36 Wraths
38 Vodka in a blue bottle
43 Millay's "___ to Silence"
44 Allen buried in Greenmount Cemetery
45 Leafy vegetable
46 Nothing to write home about
48 Eastern bloc?
51 Fossil at a Mesopotamian dig?
52 Underground treasure
53 With 86-Down, emphatic affirmative
55 Spanish gold
56 Nick and Nora's pet
57 Vietnam War copters
59 Don of morning radio
60 Lipton competitor
62 Rescue team, briefly
64 Lively party
67 Comic actress Anna
68 Kevin of *Soapdish*
69 *Tiny Alice* playwright
70 Stick in a lock
71 Cops-and-robbers "gunshot"
72 Thurman of *Henry & June*
75 Performed first
76 Ecclesiastical councils
80 Choose
81 Battles
82 Cream
85 Meal served with a ladle
86 See 53-Down
88 Albatross features
89 Unlike talkies
90 ___ coffee
91 Bill, the Science Guy
92 More socially awkward
93 Party potable
95 Flies like an eagle
96 Queen Elizabeth's spouse
97 Dolores Haze's literary nickname
100 Off-track figure
102 Boot
103 *The Lone Ranger* role
104 Try to buy
105 Stupefies
110 Galba's predecessor as emperor
113 Stocking part
114 Food label info: Abbr.
115 Lowish pinochle card
116 Remind ad nauseam
117 Investment plan, for short
118 Smidgen

GENDER BENDER by Merl Reagle

Now that's a switch!

ACROSS

1 Deserving 0 stars
6 Ox's cousin
10 Sox fan, often
15 Work on one's grammar
16 May preceder, on cable TV
17 Teatro alla Scala locale
18 Cause of tearing
19 First-time adding machine
  user's shout?
21 Darling
22 Takes to court
24 Diluted and then some
25 Where roasts roast
27 Rey of filmdom
31 First female Speaker
  of the House
33 Some eyes, once
34 School grps.
36 ___ Brith
37 Bold Ruler, to Secretariat
38 Create, as a ruckus
39 With 52-Across, what some
  words in this puzzle must
  undergo before making sense
42 Oklahoma town
44 Many, for one
45 Simone's simoleons
46 Movado competitor
48 Sleuth's shout
51 Part of a leaf
52 See 39-Across
56 Loy companion
58 Nuisance
59 Crime author Buchanan
60 Game set in a mansion
61 Formulaic
63 Distinguishing features
65 Po box, for one
67 Upset easer, for short
68 Shoat's protest
69 "___ to please"
70 Unknown, on a TV sched.
73 Inferior window material?
78 Wedding keepsake
80 Start the computer again
81 Strange-sounding lake
82 Ruth's mother-in-law
83 Dramatist Clifford
84 Fay, e.g.
85 Proverbial pit

DOWN

1 Each
2 Way's opposite
3 Limp corn chip?
4 Grp. that offered Hope
5 Convey things
6 Post-workout woes
7 Falsehoods
8 "___ luck?"
9 A tsunami is a seismic one
10 Actress Lawrence
11 "Boola Boola" singer
12 Nice-looking leg, in slang
13 The Ducks, on scoreboards
14 Cambodia's Lon ___
17 Four-time Indianapolis
  500 champ Rick
20 "Hello ___!" (old comic's
  greeting)
23 Start to form?
26 Tenor, sax
27 Aye's opposite
28 Relaying site, often
29 Ear-related
30 Grp. that got off the ground
  in the '60s
31 NewsHour airer
32 Southwest heading,
  sometimes: Abbr.
33 Toupees
35 Good to go
37 Nose-in-the-air sort
38 Some Eastern music
40 Throw
41 Jackie's "O"
42 Church chorus
43 German article
46 Sheriff's kid, on old TV
47 Elite bunch
48 2, on an ATM
49 Dutch artist Frans
50 Parched hombre's request
52 Word of honor
53 Junior moron?
54 Que. neighbor
55 "If I Ruled the World" rapper
57 Poet's night
58 Predicaments
61 Between, in brief
62 Criminal crew
63 Opening with color
64 Pay ___
66 Ding-a-lings
67 Stationed
69 "The doctor ___"
71 Ends of London
72 Athos, Porthos,
  and Aramis, e.g.
73 Dude's kin
74 Mary was one
75 Prez on a fin
76 "Just the opposite!"
77 "Odds ___ . . ."
79 R & D room

UP-SCALE by David J. Kahn

Whose theme will be revealed one step at a time.

TIME LIMIT	YOUR TIME
30 MINUTES	

ACROSS

1 Postulates
8 Press
12 Bumps
16 Frees
17 Carpet ___
18 Magazine with the column "Ask E. Jean"
19 Transition between different plant communities
20 Physician who treats weightlifters?
22 Contract for actress Russo?
24 Aristotle output
25 Pablo Neruda piece
26 Its name comes from a native word for "hippopotamus"
28 Season in 26-Across
29 Collected
33 Labor problem in Philadelphia or Denver?
38 Potential call-in participant
40 ___ party
41 Opal or topaz?
44 Clodhopper
46 Of a mind
47 *London Fields* novelist
48 Participant in a revival: Abbr.
49 DC school
50 "Granted . . ."
51 Lick
52 Kind of designer
53 Pitched weight-loss programs?
55 "___ It Goes"
57 Elimination role-playing game popular on college campuses
59 Musical performance in Vientiane?
61 Suck-ups
65 Difficulty
66 Take ___ (have some)
68 "The wise one," in a proverb
69 Unfleshed-out
73 Waiter's reaction to a big gratuity?
77 Igloo features?
79 It's noble
80 Mario ___ of the 1990s NBA champion Rockets
81 Drinks from a bowl
82 Like the ropes in tug-of-war playoffs
83 Lockbox document
84 "The even mead, that ___ brought sweetly forth": Shak.
85 Goes after, with "to"

DOWN

1 Achieva replacements
2 Bolt, in a way
3 High
4 From Valencia to Palma
5 Cathedral sight
6 Strain
7 Tick off
8 City on the Danube
9 Perfunctory
10 "I didn't know that!"
11 Does intros, tells jokes, etc.
12 Tough audience
13 Part of many an inn's name
14 Snatch
15 Ticks, for short
21 State revenue sources
23 Keen
27 One may be seen . . . or heard . . . at a theater
30 "___ well"
31 Poet's contraction
32 First name in skin care
34 Fishing equipment
35 Words of empathy
36 Over
37 Some costume designs
39 Copper-zinc alloy
41 Calamitous
42 "Built better than it has to be" sloganeer
43 *Get Shorty* actor Delroy ___
45 Light and melodramatic
49 Start fighting
50 Altoids holders
52 Not clear
53 Bygone satellites: Abbr.
54 Come to nothing
56 Badly burned
58 Sailor's acquisition
60 0%
62 Trough
63 Crate
64 Source of some mushrooms, for short
67 Fastest of a noted trio
69 Got rid of
70 Scratch
71 Water surrounding South Bass Island
72 Mark Antony's love
74 Paella ingredients
75 Arrange
76 Beginning to skid?
78 One circumnavigated the globe in under 31 hrs. 28 mins.

SUB-MERGING by Patrick Merrell

In which "sub" can precede each half of the answer to each asterisked clue.

ACROSS

1   Stunts are often performed on it
9   Literary collection
12 Dry's opposite
16 Completed, as coloring books
17 *Line on a bill
19 *Askance
20 Presenting, as a star
21 Common locale for a 1-Across
22 Belt holder
23 Handkerchief, perhaps
24 *Fighting force
30 Astronomer Hale and others
31 Tidy sum
32 Callaloo ingredient
36 Aeolian creation
37 *What a sheet of ice may provide
41 Barely acceptable
43 Father of Cronos
44 Dust collector
45 Just
46 Volume unit
48 Govt. procurement agcy.
49 Like cassette tapes
51 Mitsubishi SUV's
53 *Homo erectus, e.g.
56 French quarters
58 US
59 Not by download, say
60 Cool red giant
61 *Like British society, famously
66 A mean Amin
69 Volunteer's declaration
70 Crossing pair
71 Unwelcome
73 *Sugarless product
77 *Prescribed manner
78 House features pioneered by Frank Lloyd Wright
79 Like the road taken
80 "Epithalamium" or "Prothalamium"
81 Obscurers, in an idiom

DOWN

1   Overseas cans
2   Name that means "lion" in Hebrew
3   Hair
4   It's found in a pencil
5   Mountain ashes
6   Cad
7   Worked (up)
8   SSN's, e.g.
9   Inclined
10 Just as dense
11 Warning in the game Go
12 Prior
13 Cat's "copy"
14 Selene's counterpart
15 Boxman
18 Mars: Prefix
24 Possessed
25 Component of bauxite
26 Checked someone's arrest history
27 "___ thee"
28 Cousin of a rebec
29 With 47-Down, zip
33 So-called "Charlemagne of Germany"
34 *The Merry Jesters* artist, 1906
35 Amphora handle
37 Criticizes wittily
38 Photo lab abbr.
39 Some wedding guests
40 An official language of the Northwest Territories
42 "Quit your joshin'!"
44 ___ Men (Grammy-winning group)
46 Possible response to "But you already have it"
47 See 29-Down
50 ___ de Triomphe
51 Turn-of-the-century year in Edward I's reign
52 Circuit board component
54 Put forth
55 Pull in
57 74-Down takers: Abbr.
60 Series of lines
62 East River crosser in NYC
63 *Dona Flor and Her Two Husbands* author
64 Newswoman O'Donnell
65 Arm of Napoleon
66 Washington Univ. ___ Louis
67 Action figure
68 Liking
72 Last word in Biden's presidential oath
73 10/
74 Test with an analytical writing section: Abbr.
75 Mountain West Conference player
76 Lit. output

YOU'RE SOLVING . . . WITH WHAT?
by Brendan Emmett Quigley

Soon you'll understand what we're referring to.

ACROSS

1 Religious hermitages
8 Wet season
13 Skip Day participants: Abbr.
16 Hot, sweet drink
17 "Exceed your vision" sloganeer
18 Switzerland's ___ de Neuchâtel
19 Go, with 76-Across
20 Damn, with 52-Across
22 Member of la famille
23 Buck ___, first African American coach in Major League Baseball
25 Triumphant shout
26 ___ defense (chess opening)
27 Handle, with 74-Across
29 Temple pilasters
31 Water ___, Inc.
32 Latin phrase that may accompany John and Jane Doe
35 Arguer
38 Rialto sign
41 Pass, with 61-Across
44 Match
46 Link's destination
47 Dummkopfs
49 Open-bolt weapons
50 Work in volumes: Abbr.
52 See 20-Across
54 Series extreme
55 Bridge opening
57 ___ Stanley, 1920s singer known as the Phonograph Girl
58 Sales pitch?
59 Capital celebrating its 1,000th anniversary in 2010
61 See 41-Across
67 Wall-to-wall
71 Time it takes mountains to form
72 Knowing
73 Universal
74 See 27-Across
76 See 19-Across
78 Picnic supply
79 They're found on the range
80 Joan of Arc, e.g.
81 NC's capital
82 Sculpture subject
83 Scratched

DOWN

1 Insurance co. records
2 Bar at a resort?
3 William ___, half of the team that produced Tom and Jerry and Yogi Bear
4 Lowland created by plate tectonics
5 Stick ___ in the water
6 Jean Lafitte's milieu
7 Appetizer often served with chutney
8 Change in a government-set exchange rate
9 Almost nothing, in poker
10 Cord fiber
11 Logician's word
12 It may be seen in chains
13 Guardian Angels founder Curtis
14 Remover of handlebars
15 What a director directs
21 Spoon
24 Prenuptial?
27 Hotel founder J. Willard Marriott, e.g.
28 Copy
30 Annual competition first won by the Temple Owls, for short
32 City near Oberhausen
33 "___ so!"
34 Horse's head?
35 Part of un año
36 Battlin'
37 Stimulate
38 Oscar-winning director Templeton
39 Don't call, maybe
40 Tabloid twin's name
42 Teeming
43 ___ impulse
45 Get to enter
48 Goes over
51 Opening at a laundromat
53 2016 Olympics host
56 Item for a photog
58 Sound pulse
59 Tube knob: Abbr.
60 ___ Now, 1968 gold album
61 One sleeping on a bed of nails, e.g.
62 Olympus rival
63 It gets high in the mountains
64 Head-light wearer
65 Buck for a song?
66 It might pull a calf
68 Spookily illuminated, perhaps
69 Director of the Man with No Name trilogy
70 Called on the range
73 Mr. T's last name
75 Naples's historic Castell dell'___
77 New Test. book

CROSSOVER HITS by Mike Shenk

And the place is jumping!

ACROSS

1 Colonial address
6 State representative
10 Be mean
15 "Cold, ungenial is the ___ . . .": Shelley
16 Polynesian performances
18 Cal Neva Resort setting
19 1967 hit for the Turtles
21 1980 hit for Bette Midler
22 Abrupt removal from the board
23 One may make the grade
25 Officially choose
26 She "made a fool of everyone," in a Beatles song
27 Angel Clare's wife
28 Key letters
30 One flying in a cloud, perhaps
32 1966 hit for the Monkees
37 1977 hit for Barbra Streisand
42 Grave
43 They may be held with an Italian grip
45 *The Last Don* star
46 Pulls down
48 Culture confirmation
50 Goes up against
51 Countless
53 Tiptoe, say
55 Movie theater
56 1933 hit for Ted Lewis
58 1995 hit for Mariah Carey & Boyz II Men
60 Bessemer process byproduct
62 *The Black Stallion* boy
63 Places to take notes
67 Union acquisition?
69 Simple
74 Civil War buff, perhaps
76 Both mother and wife of Oedipus
77 1980 hit for Supertramp
78 2004 hit for Green Day
80 Ruby's partner
81 Title for a lord of Lourdes
82 Nascar driver Hamlin
83 Line holders
84 Inhabitants of the Temple of Isis
85 Walkway definer

DOWN

1 Either end of America
2 N.H.L. coach Vigneault
3 Pack : wolf :: bloat : ___
4 Winner of the 2003 Cooper-Hewitt Lifetime Achievement Award
5 Etta James portrayer in *Cadillac Records*
6 Discharge from the infantry
7 Docking aid
8 Prince Valiant's wife
9 Unlikely to offend
10 Scale interval
11 Golden number
12 Optimistic utterance
13 Famous foundling
14 Sources of some pressure
17 Oblation setting
20 Astronomer H. P., discoverer of comets
24 Tony nominee for the 1993 revival of *Anna Christie*
26 Cold showers
29 Rent places
31 Work-week cheer
32 Consummate
33 Car that made its world debut at the 1989 Chicago Auto Show
34 Ingrediente del paella
35 Upper
36 Novelist upon whose work 1957's Best Picture was based
38 Start, say
39 His horse was Babieca
40 *The Vampire Diaries* heroine
41 Compulsively curious
44 It takes two to do it
47 Sorrowful sounds
49 Pivoting machine part
52 Derived from one of the Bs
54 Digging
57 36-Down's birthplace
59 Rainforest concern
61 Short-lived spinoff of 1982
63 Fire
64 Serving short sentences?
65 Cabinet resignee of 1988
66 Member of the genus *Helix*
68 Constellation between Perseus and Cetus
70 Not so bright
71 Not clean
72 Skipper on the water
73 Pan companion
75 Quadrennial straw poll city
76 They may be jam-packed
79 Green feature

GOING UNDERGROUND by Patrick Blindauer

Follow the tunnels made by five creatures to complete this pesky puzzle.

ACROSS

1 Like *The Wizard of Oz*, notably
8 Open piece of real estate
11 It's uplifting
15 Theme song of Milton Berle
16 __ Pince, librarian at Hogwarts
18 Sound
19 1958 Curtis/Poitier film
20 Members of the family Hydrophidae
22 Succession
23 Hugo-winning writer Timothy
25 Close up, in a way
26 Chinese zodiac figure
29 Barnyard sounds
31 —
32 Politician once a judge on *The People's Court*
35 Unthinkingly, after "on"
36 Cluster
37 North, e.g.
39 —
42 Host of VH1's *Rap School*
43 Discontinue
47 "Doing ju-u-ust fine"
51 What the binary number for two looks like
52 Snap
54 Pussy foot
55 Visually assesses
57 Bible locale?
58 Go for
59 Jell-O specialty
61 —
63 Stream blocker
66 Home, to Helmut
70 The "Ted" of *Ted, White, and Blue*
71 Crib
72 Turns away
74 Memory unit, briefly
75 "You cheated!"
77 Bring up
79 I.P.O. of 1998
83 Mildly enjoyed, as a joke
85 —
88 Sent a quick note, nowadays
89 Arrogance, slangily
90 Before
91 Polo of *Meet the Fockers*
92 —
93 Slight

DOWN

1 Describing JFK: Abbr.
2 Pop hit of the 1920s
3 City near D-Day beaches
4 Ironic way to eat in
5 Oven cleaner ingredient
6 Punchee's exclamation
7 Pablo ___ Picasso
8 One known as the "supreme soul"
9 Childish comeback
10 Org. with annual awards once presented at the Grand Ole Opry House
11 "I heard ___!"
12 Actor Scott
13 Bygone Oldsmobiles
14 Zeroes
17 ___ secy.
21 Delta ___ (*Legally Blonde* characters)
24 Jolson's real first name
27 Do
28 Part of a cry during a raid
30 Bouncing baby of books
32 Best
33 Far from certain
34 New England's ___ State College
36 Communiqué: Abbr.
38 State where Kool-Aid was invented: Abbr.
40 *In Too Deep* actress
41 Modem terminals?
44 "That's the rub!"
45 ___-Seal (waterproofing brand)
46 Throw back, as some tuna
48 Hold forth
49 Like a Derbyshire chair
50 Fixated (on)
52 Something you'll get a kick out of
53 Tokyo-based IT giant
56 "My dear ___"
58 Signed in, say
60 Day of the week named for Mjölnir's owner: Abbr.
62 French pronoun
63 Ad-lib
64 Very big, in Bourges
65 Less certain
67 Place with lots of slots
68 Agreed
69 1-Down way to travel, once
72 "___ pulls angels out of Heaven": John Bunyan
73 ___ à porter
76 The King's followers?
78 *In Too Deep* actor
80 Plane, informally
81 Pot seed
82 *Son of Frankenstein* role
84 Call by another name
86 Modern business info
87 It may be loaded

TAKE FIVE by Patrick Blindauer

But take each one only once.

ACROSS

1 One of about a billion believers
6 Drop down?
10 Ran into
16 Bagel choice
17 Word that may come before itself?
18 *Airplane!* heroine
19 *Macbeth* prop
21 Pet toy filling
22 Some buglers
23 Rossi of *Sons of Anarchy*
24 "Rhythm ___ Dancer" (1992 Snap! song)
26 Cover
27 Common word that's sometimes contracted
28 Group with primates
31 Snap, maybe
34 Wanting for nothing
35 As easy as falling off ___
36 A hose comes out of it
38 Poetic time of day
40 Triangular part of a house
44 Waggle dance waggler
45 Get absorbed
47 Postal label
48 First name in the Motorcycle Hall of Fame
50 Figure set by the Federal Reserve
52 *Forever*, ___ (1996 humor book)
53 Suburb of Boston
55 Timorous
57 ___ the Clown
58 Neighborhood of New Orleans
59 Rock band?
60 Oscar-winning actress who is a practicing 1-Across
62 Stuff in a muffin, maybe
64 When repeated, a *Teletubbies* character
66 Wipe out
67 Lightheaded people?
71 Bump hard
72 Course for beginners?
73 Certain game win
74 "Just joshing"
76 Film fx
79 Rant about, slangily
81 Washington and others
84 Wait on
85 It's waved at the Olympics
86 Vehicle with a hyphen in its name
87 Passes, with "away"
88 Source of the word "brogue"
89 Didn't disturb

DOWN

1 She wrote the line "His truth is marching on"
2 Like some flights: Abbr.
3 Cause for a Band-Aid
4 Animated exclamation
5 Frees, in a way
6 Pack ___
7 High, in a way
8 Photocopier tray abbr.
9 Do, musically
10 Product displacement?
11 With 37-Down, menu phrase
12 What the Australian TV show *Blankety Blanks* was based on
13 Trivial
14 Tech debut of 1946
15 Asset for a team
20 "Voi ___ sapete" (*Le Nozze di Figaro* song)
25 Hour, day, or week
27 Writer Rand
29 Hailee nominated for an Oscar for *True Grit*
30 Parts of some wheels
31 First king of all England
32 Cordial sign-off
33 Top tube
34 Facial spots
37 See 11-Down
39 ___'acte
41 *My Name Is* ___ (1965 gold album)
42 Caps
43 March on
46 1981 automotive debut
47 Power provider: Abbr.
49 Certain zest
51 Eastern pooh-bah
54 Bawl (out)
56 Ghastly
59 Capital in the Østlandet district
61 [Shiver]
63 They take 20 to 30 years to mature
65 Popular parts of platters
67 Dismissive exclamation
68 Reluctant
69 First half of an ice cream flavor
70 Like some credit cards
71 "Chase the Pig," for one
75 Shank's end
76 Pas de ___ (ballet jump)
77 Eats
78 Thomas More's Utopia, e.g.
80 Together
82 Media inits. since 1970
83 ___ End

Round 4:
PLAYOFFS

TESTING, TESTING, 1, 2, 3 . . . by Stanley Newman

A playoff challenge that's unusually fine . . . or, as the explosives expert might say, "4-Down!"

SET A

ACROSS

1 Lead character in *Glengarry Glen Ross*
9 Epiphany VIP
15 "Hercules" or "Samson"
16 Very high
17 Takes first
18 Dwarfs
19 Long account
20 For most people
22 Luau, often
24 There's no interest in them
27 *Iliad* messenger
28 Secesh
31 Low-level
32 Right after
33 Random number generators
34 Kennedy's successor
36 Two-Oscar actor
38 Lacking water
39 Birds do it
41 Ace, almost always
42 It's close to 1
43 Don
44 Male opera role sung by mezzo-sopranos
45 It may get you 58-Across
48 Firebrand, perhaps
50 Dictionary listing
54 Butters up high
55 Capital raised from scratch
57 Silver, for one
58 See 45-Across
59 Eye or nose, essentially
60 Sharks' habitat

DOWN

1 Buffaloes
2 Price lines
3 Gut reaction
4 See blurb
5 Coat
6 Draws for some customers
7 Amethyst cousin
8 Aurora's state
9 City network
10 Where some aisles end
11 Fast jet
12 Hood ornaments
13 Put (up)
14 Lie
21 Spring up
23 Extensions of a sort
24 Round alternative
25 Ruins
26 Grammy Lifetime Achievement Award recipient of 1987
29 ___ Polytechnique
30 Carpenter's tool
32 Grand Slam part
33 Book subtitled *The Modern Science of Mental Health*
35 1964 Beatles tune
37 Caddies hold them
40 Stringed instrument
43 Open one's eyes
44 Ride
46 Michener epic
47 Einstein's onetime home
48 Rose ___
49 Rose Mary Murphy's love
51 Race introduced in England in 1895
52 Outside
53 Not natural
56 Fixed

SET B

ACROSS

1 What Genesis starts with
9 Ancient stargazer
15 "Messiah," for one
16 Style of skiing
17 Beats everybody
18 Publicity devices
19 Long story
20 Book category
22 First of the Annette Funicello/Frankie Avalon films
24 Government paper
27 Pupil's locale
28 Yank's opponent
31 Fundamental
32 Well briefed about
33 Rear-view mirror accessories
34 Olympic Airways founder
36 Poirot portrayer
38 "That's great!"
39 Shed one's skin
41 Postal Service symbol
42 PC button
43 Mob leader
44 Humperdinck hero
45 Diamond datum
48 Vile firebrand
50 Semester
54 Some mountain climbers
55 Capital city since 1960
57 Copyright violator
58 Halfway home
59 Motion detector, e.g.
60 Where Broadway is

DOWN

1 Intimidates
2 Cantata excerpt
3 Sign of distress
4 See blurb
5 Get dressed, with "up"
6 Flavor enhancers
7 New Hampshire's state flower
8 Olympian character
9 Furnace connections
10 Some shrines
11 Sudden outburst
12 Hand jewelry
13 Deal preceder
14 Final group
21 Begin budding
23 Building extensions
24 Beef buy
25 Ruinations
26 Longtime Carnegie Hall president
29 Arles academy
30 Angled cut
32 PGA event
33 Scientology philosophy
35 Beatles hit with the lyric "My tears are falling like rain from the sky"
37 Often-blended drinks
40 Hood's weapon
43 Reach
44 Get on
46 New nation of 1836
47 European capital
48 They may hold your pants up
49 Anne Nichols title hero
51 *The Time Machine* race
52 Protective coat
53 All sewn up
56 All sewn up

SET C

ACROSS

1 Symbol on a General Mills cereal box
9 One of the Wise Men
15 Form similar to opera
16 Like Mont Blanc
17 Earns the top medal
18 Film doubles may perform them
19 Heroic narrative
20 Paperback book category
22 Surfside gathering
24 Short-term government securities, for short
27 Flower painted by van Gogh
28 Soldier in gray
31 Kind of metabolism
32 Familiar with
33 They're spotted in casinos
34 Greek shipping magnate
36 Peter who portrayed Poirot
38 In good order
39 Lose feathers
41 Golf coup
42 Upper-left keyboard key
43 Gangster boss
44 Grimm boy
45 Diamond theft
48 Spreader of prejudice
50 Six years for a senator
54 Mountain goats
55 South American capital
57 Maritime marauder
58 Halfway around the bases
59 Detection device
60 Slice of the Big Apple

DOWN

1 Dairy farm dwellers
2 Diva's showcase
3 Hungry feeling
4 Enthusiastic remark
5 Dress (up)
6 Scents
7 Purplish
8 Status of Zeus or Mercury
9 Utility pipelines
10 Wedding locales
11 Gush
12 Little-finger jewelry
13 Poker ritual
14 Take a break
21 Start to grow
23 Right-angle shapes
24 Steak order
25 Bugaboos
26 Violinist who helped save Carnegie Hall
29 French place of education
30 Angled edge
32 Major tennis tourney
33 L. Ron Hubbard book
35 Schlub's lament
37 Afternoon socials
40 Robin Hood weapon
43 Wake up
44 Drive bananas
46 State that was once a country
47 City on the Aar
48 What hula dancers shake
49 Irish Rose's lover on Broadway
51 *The Time Machine* race
52 Citrus peel
53 Built
56 Complete collection

LANGUAGE IMMERSION by Bob Klahn

A handsome interlock of familiar words and phrases with teasing clues.

SET A

ACROSS

1 Get a line on
6 Finally understands
15 Party leader
16 Pop-up ad, e.g.
17 Unbroken
18 Bit of paronomasia
19 *Peer Gynt* character
20 They follow orders
21 Short pan
22 Boom attachment
23 Author who wrote "America is my country, and Paris is my hometown"
25 Native American tribe that assisted the US in the Civil War
27 Sandburg's "___ Window"
28 Tendrils, in botany
29 Put the arm on
30 Visual image, perhaps
32 Joined forces?
34 Broadway's *For Colored Girls Who Have Considered Suicide / When the Rainbow Is* ___
36 Goes in the right direction
37 Caused bad blood at the clinic?
41 It's marked by bands of quartz and feldspar
45 Opening
46 Almost catch
48 Once yclept
49 No longer available
50 Memorable hurricane of 1961
51 1: Abbr.
52 Life force
53 Links locale
54 Attachments of a sort
56 Apt to blow at any time
59 Bass role in *Fidelio*
60 Politer than polite
61 Mouth
62 Military camp sights
63 Long-winded

DOWN

1 Lead-in to a cross-over hit?
2 Inactive title-holders
3 Flipper
4 Flipper holder
5 Snake carving?
6 Mozart or Haydn
7 Use a Ouija board
8 Beautiful
9 Largest known dwarf planet in the solar system
10 Explorer, e.g.
11 "Home away from home" grp.
12 Provocative
13 Real poser
14 It's hard to solve Rubik's Cube with this
24 Two-leaved pedestal table
25 Persian
26 Pool term that literally means "hammered"
31 Reading unit
33 OK
35 Not open
37 Actor whom Ebert called "the soul of film noir"
38 Strapped
39 First British colony in the West Indies
40 Assamese or Cantonese
42 Adds
43 Mary Todd Lincoln organized several at the White House
44 Organoleptic
47 African families
53 Horatio or Claudius
55 Trace
57 Big hits: Abbr.
58 Down

SET B

ACROSS

1 Lab checker
6 Sees through at last
15 Roast ham?
16 Encroachment
17 Wild
18 Mercutio's "Ask for me tomorrow, and you shall find me a grave man," e.g.
19 Ibsen's Mountain King, for one
20 Members of an order
21 Reaction to goo
22 Word with inner, outer, or flying
23 Ale holder
25 Boys Town locale
27 ___ minimum
28 Clouds composed of ice crystals
29 Took "downtown"
30 Matrix graphic
32 Prepared to serve
34 Ample, informally
36 Thug's thous
37 Made a key mistake
41 Layered rock
45 It's a start
46 Bite a bit
48 Originally
49 Carried away
50 She served beers on *Cheers*
51 "Miami Vice Theme" composer Hammer
52 X
53 Sub-assembly site
54 Some claims
56 Having a short fuse
59 *Fidelio* jailer
60 Like Miss Congeniality
61 Total
62 Where grunts grab grub
63 Too talkative

DOWN

1 Rocky connection
2 Distinguished retirees
3 Well-balanced person
4 Close up tight
5 North America's deepest river gorge
6 Frank
7 ___ within (old sign)
8 Like Tasers in use
9 Olympic troublemaker
10 Navigator or Pathfinder
11 Hope provider during WWII: Abbr.
12 Spicy
13 Difficult situation
14 Clapping with this is very hard
24 Tilt
25 Colorful cover
26 Billiards stroke
31 Length of London
33 Like some briefs
35 Like some yards
37 *Farewell, My Lovely* star, 1975
38 Far behind, betting-wise
39 One of the Lesser Antilles
40 Local talk
42 Adds, as humor
43 They take place in the dark
44 Kind of overload
47 Safari sightings
53 Soma Cube inventor Piet Hein, for one
55 Tittle
57 Time divs.
58 Take a course?

SET C

ACROSS

1 It checks Rex
6 Gets smart about
15 Roast host
16 Forced entry
17 Untamed
18 Play on words
19 Dweller under a bridge, in folklore
20 Mother superior's inferiors
21 "Gr-r-ross!"
22 Three-sided sail
23 *The Autobiography of Alice B. Toklas* writer
25 Nebraska city named for an Native American tribe
27 "___ price you can afford"
28 Wispy white clouds
29 Arrested
30 Image composed of binary data
32 Joined the Army, e.g.
34 Plenty, in Podunk
36 $1,000 bills, slangily
37 Made a keyboard error
41 Laminated metamorphic rock
45 Beginning bars
46 Try to bite
48 Born, in a bridal bio
49 Confiscated
50 *Cheers* waitress
51 Dean's "Surf City" partner
52 "The Sweetheart of Sigma ___"
53 It stocks lox
54 Property encumbrances
56 Quick-tempered
59 Boxer Marciano, at birth
60 Super-sweet, as a personality
61 Out-and-out
62 Boot camp meal sites
63 Full of hot air

DOWN

1 Part of a one-two
2 Some retired professors
3 Circus performer
4 Circus performer
5 Idaho/Oregon wilderness area
6 Hot dog
7 Ask questions
8 Strikingly beautiful
9 Goddess of strife
10 Yukon or Explorer, for short
11 Entertain-the-troops grp.
12 Agreeably pungent
13 Difficult puzzle
14 What "washes the other," in a phrase
24 Tilt toward the sky
25 Colorful floor cover
26 Tricky billiards shot
31 39+ inches in England
33 Photocopier paper option
35 Enclosed, as a field
37 Robert of *The Night of the Hunter*
38 Burdened with debt
39 ___ and Nevis (Caribbean nation)
40 Language offshoot
42 Gives a hypo
43 These might raise your spirits
44 Part of ESP
47 Groups of lions
53 Copenhagener, e.g.
55 Kappa preceder
57 Nolte's *48___*
58 "___ my shorts!" (Bart Simpson cry)

ROUTE 66 by Patrick Berry

The final leg of the 31-Across to the championship

SET A

ACROSS

1 Fantasy home?
7 Growing business's asset
15 In the US and Canada it begins with "O"
16 Basic
17 Far-sighted vision?
18 Becomes a new person, say
19 Chopin's *Nocturne in ___*
20 1960s TV series cowritten by Mel Brooks
21 Don Juan type
22 Firearm measure
24 Historic region east of Paris
25 Had a few seconds
26 Tube fare?
27 1864's Battle of ___ Creek
28 What's on Medusa's mind?
30 Lays at one's doorstep
31 [See blurb]
32 Advanced
33 In silence
36 Hershey's brand
40 Hands and feet
41 Items in stock
42 Lightweight boxer
43 Derby sight
44 Publication eligible for an Akatsuka Award
45 Hopper
46 Closing
48 Actor on the original *Star Trek*
50 Applaud
51 Grant
52 ___ Republic of Uruguay (Uruguay's official name)
53 Connect
54 London hotel features
55 First host of *The Late Late Show*

DOWN

1 Universal needs
2 Fire up
3 One who's going to anger management
4 Great Scot
5 Construction company?
6 Big pickle
7 Safe crackers?
8 Maintain
9 Work on one's figure, say
11 Worked one's way up
12 ___ Baroni, opera singer in *A Night at the Opera*
13 Fighting for freedom, maybe
14 Hounds
23 Play money?
26 Sounds from a steeple
27 Brewery supply
29 Phony
30 They're tied at the top
32 Nefarious group
33 Collar snap?
34 Ignorant
35 "What angel wakes me from my flowery bed?" speaker
36 Onetime invaders of Baghdad
37 Coming soon
38 "Dat's my boy dat said dat" speaker
39 Word often preceded in irony by "big"
41 Miniature
44 Coat of arms component
45 In anger
47 ___-Tibetan
49 Heavy brace

SET B

ACROSS

1 Knight spot?
7 Beans or corn
15 Something to stand for
16 Like bleach
17 Las Vegas hotel/casino, with "the"
18 Assumes a role
19 Key of Elgar's *Cello Concerto*
20 Sitcom with the catchphrase "Would you believe . . . ?"
21 Tool with teeth
22 Shotgun measure
24 Unpasteurized milk product
25 Took as a loss, informally
26 Pasta variety
27 Symbol on Lebanon's flag
28 Medusa's "hair"
30 Odd tunes for June
31 [See blurb]
32 Tudor emblem
33 Without a word
36 Chocolate-and-caramel candy
40 Rental properties
41 Skull's partner
42 Result of littering?
43 Money from admissions
44 Comics genre
45 "A Wild ___" (early Bugs Bunny cartoon)
46 Last appearance
48 Scott's portrayer on *Star Trek*
50 Sing the praises of
51 Reach
52 Like Kashmir rugs
53 Be sympathetic (to)
54 Facilities with cups and saucers
55 Beat poet Gary or film director Zack

DOWN

1 What cell phones often double as
2 Able to move
3 Gong accessory
4 "Your face, my ___, is a book . . .": "Macbeth"
5 Block lettering
6 Medical drama of 1970s TV
7 Noisy toys
8 Declare positively
9 Awkward shoe for walking
10 ___ Code (1930s–'60s filmmaking guidelines)
11 Ascended with difficulty
12 Ricky or Lucy
13 Awaiting a judgment
14 Bedevils
23 Pot plant?
26 Sounds of laughter
27 Holders of spirits
29 Aspirant to the throne
30 Top score sharers
32 Suitor's purchase
33 Inherently unflattering photo
34 Obliviously
35 Largest moon of Uranus
36 Builders of the world's largest contiguous empire
37 Not much further along
38 Ragtime Jimmy of old Vaudeville
39 "Big ___" (song from *Sweet Charity*)
41 Chicken shrimp?
44 Latin phrase, often
45 With indignation
47 ___-Soviet relations
49 Draft choices

SET C

ACROSS

1 King's home
7 Marketable farm commodity
15 Country song?
16 Having a pH higher than 7
17 Thirsty person's vision of water, maybe
18 Engages in make-believe
19 Key with one sharp
20 Old sitcom with the catchphrase "Sorry about that, Chief"
21 Autumn tool
22 Instrument panel component
24 Cheese with a white coating
25 Snacked on
26 Tubular pasta
27 Moth-repelling wood
28 Snakes and such
30 Holiday album standards
31 [See blurb]
32 Flower with thorns
33 Without saying a word
36 Chocolate-covered caramels sold in theaters
40 Measuring stick divisions
41 Femur and fibula
42 Young seal
43 Moveable fence part
44 Graphic novels from Japan
45 Loser to the tortoise
46 Farewell performance
48 *Star Trek* actor James
50 Acknowledge the quality of
51 Stretch out
52 From the East
53 Tell, as a story
54 Afternoon eateries in Britain
55 TV host Tom

DOWN

1 The house in *Big Brother* has lots of them
2 Work on a Pixar film
3 One walking off the job
4 Macbeth, for one
5 Denmark-based toy company
6 Reason to call 911
7 Toys in cops and robbers
8 State without proof
9 Glide on ice
10 *Airplane!* actor Robert
11 Clumsily ascended
12 Actor Montalbán
13 Up before a judge
14 Incessantly annoys
23 Feed the kitty
26 Bell tower sounds
27 Wine barrels
29 "The Great ___" (1955 Platters hit)
30 Ones sharing the presidency, say
32 Prizefight venue
33 Picture taken at a police station
34 Not cognizant
35 Oberon's wife
36 Genghis Khan's army
37 In a mile or two, say
38 Jimmy with a large proboscis
39 One actively shopping
41 Publishing house with a rooster logo
44 "In God We Trust," for one
45 How angry replies are delivered
47 Chinese: Prefix
49 Plow pullers

TALENT SHOW by Mike Shenk

It's "Open Mike" time at the ACPT.

SET A

ACROSS

1 Flower's bud
6 Checking account?
15 Dome prototype
16 Punctuation with four digits
17 Angle's complement
18 Ones known for their old tricks
19 Slug sign
20 Athanaël's convert
21 Pussycat Dolls hit "Don't ___"
22 Larousse entry
23 Forward
25 Hope strongly
26 Jalapeño biter's desire
28 Attenborough or Olivier
29 National currency coin with a hole in the middle
30 Caruso show
32 Tight
33 Set down
34 Her characters include Jondalar and Echozar
35 Velvet Revolution setting
38 Literally, "resplendent island"
42 Not so well done
43 Hair splitter
44 Ones who believe in spirits
45 Decides
46 1940 Marx Brothers film
48 Monk's specialty
49 Scanner file extension
50 Doesn't play well
51 Effusive, colloquially
53 Excised
55 Nabisco brand
56 Without warning
57 Free address choice
58 "No, you're right"
59 Lost one's balance

DOWN

1 Chief
2 Spot for four colons
3 Scrap
4 Sloop part
5 Exclusive
6 Acts the exorcist
7 Casual greeting
8 You might see a page on one
9 Army swimmer
10 Some grade school homework
11 Right-minded org.?
12 Made a retraction, maybe
13 Result of rumination
14 Tackled
24 Chuck's sister, on NBC's *Chuck*
25 Heading for the bar?
27 Gnomes
29 Pitcher of hits
31 Photoshop filter choice
32 Business execs
34 One in a pinch
35 Cowboys, e.g.
36 In a wink
37 One unlikely to open wide
38 Equivalent of two fins
39 The Tarantula and the Crab
40 Grammy winner for the country song "Hold Me"
41 It ends at the shoulder
43 Los Angeles suburb
46 Topic for actors working as waiters
47 Bites
50 Book entries
52 Difficulty in walking
54 Chi preceder

SET B

ACROSS

1 Title character who "came into the world in the middle of the thicket"
6 Board activity
15 Gibson garnish
16 Speaker's irony indicator
17 Germanic foe of Charlemagne
18 Some *Tom Jones* characters
19 Repulsive sort
20 Courtesan who sings "L'amour est une vertu rare"
21 Chinese tea
22 Entrée de dictionnaire
23 Forward, as mail
25 What you might do after you put your hands together
26 Rio makeup
28 Exclamation of surprise
29 Danish denomination
30 ABC debut of September 1993
32 Like some prunes
33 Perched
34 *The Shelters of Stone* writer
35 Capital that's reputedly home to the world's biggest castle
38 Island once known as Serendip
42 More collectable
43 Divide
44 Prohibition foes
45 Is decisive
46 Famous bit of 19th-century advice
48 Cool jazz forerunner
49 Hi-res cousin of a .jpg
50 Foul plays?
51 Enthusing, poetically
53 Struck from a story
55 ___ Wafers
56 Simultaneously
57 Google offering
58 Apologetic utterance
59 Beat

DOWN

1 Big kahuna
2 SAT challenge
3 Fight
4 Mike support
5 Private
6 Gets rid of
7 Statement accompanying a wave
8 Trip to the dry cleaner, e.g.
9 Ink jet producer?
10 Additional results
11 Grant grp.
12 Was humiliated, in a way
13 Flammable gas
14 Had a go at
24 Greenwich who cowrote "Leader of the Pack"
25 Many a poli sci student's program
27 Proverbs
29 Big name in song compilations
31 Hazy recollection
32 Deck divisions
34 Person with a booking
35 Thunder or Lightning, e.g.
36 Like mad
37 Many an indie
38 Where to see Hamilton's mug
39 Astronomers' discoveries
40 CMA's 1988 Female Vocalist of the Year
41 You might make a lot with it
43 California's ___ College
46 "He won't come this evening but surely tomorrow"
47 Pungent smells
50 Pool builders?
52 Hobbling gait
54 End of a rum cocktail

TIME LIMIT | YOUR TIME
15 MINUTES

ACROSS

1 Disney film set in a forest
6 A mate ends it
15 Burger topper
16 Gesture made with twitching fingers
17 Anglo-___
18 Tarts
19 Ooze
20 Massenet opera based on an Anatole France novel
21 When repeated, a hip-swaying dance
22 Le ___ juste
23 Dispatch once more
25 Address Allah, say
26 Juan's water
28 Manor man
29 Norwegian money
30 TV series set in the 15th Precinct
32 Fretted
33 Dismounted
34 Jean who wrote the "Earth's Children" series
35 European capital on the Vltava River
38 Ceylon, today
42 Pinker in the middle
43 Audition goal
44 Dampens
45 Chooses
46 Bit of famous old advice to a "young man"
48 Be-___
49 File name extension for some hi-res images
50 Long passes
51 Spurting, quaintly
53 On the cutting room floor
55 Nabisco's ___ Wafers
56 Suddenly
57 Google's messaging service
58 "I must have gotten it wrong"
59 Bushed

DOWN

1 Head honcho
2 Comparison
3 Brawl
4 Detonation sound
5 Close to the heart
6 Ejects
7 "Howdy!"
8 Gofer's assignment
9 Cuttlefish's cousin
10 Tallies
11 Dem. opposers
12 Admitted one's error
13 Natural gas component
14 Tried
24 J. R.'s mother on *Dallas*
25 Future attorney's study
27 Maxims
29 Old late-night hawker of records
31 Get fuzzy?
32 Hearts and spades
34 One in handcuffs, perhaps
35 League member
36 Lickety-split
37 Movie likely to wow critics more than the masses
38 Ten-spot
39 Gaseous clouds
40 Country singer who uses her first two initials
41 Road surface
43 City east of Los Angeles
46 Theatrical no-show
47 Distinctive flavors
50 Wagers
52 Halting gait, informally
54 ___ chi (martial art)

WELL-CONNECTED by Mike Nothnagel

An open construction with crossing 15-letter answers makes for a fine, final, all-round test of solving skills.

SET A

ACROSS

1 Prepared
9 Stark
15 Fully briefed
16 Figure in *The Greatest Game Ever Played*
17 Buck-passer's statement
19 Clever people have big ones
20 Towers in a harbor?
21 It might include mgs. of Mg
22 Onetime CSA member
23 Plate of fish?
25 Masseur's target
26 Small purchase
28 Pity
29 Letters of resolution?: Abbr.
31 Speaker of the House under Jackson and Van Buren
32 Listing on paper?
33 Smooth
35 *A Theologico-Political Treatise* author, 1670
36 Succeed
37 Cut off, in a way
38 Part of many rates
39 Intimate
40 Phrase that attracts consumers
42 Place for singles to gather
43 Tribe once divided into the Thervingi and Greuthungi
44 Jaw holder
47 Chemical suffix
48 Changed locks
49 San ___ (suburb of San Francisco)
50 Act like Bruce Wayne
54 "Fine by me"
55 1964 Lennon/McCartney song
56 Appropriate
57 Like some pickup games

DOWN

1 Charge when a job is done?
2 Antistrophe follower
3 "Listen!"
4 Something sharp in the kitchen
5 Grocery brand since the 1980s
6 Figure at home
7 SW Colorado's ___ Mountain
8 Athlete's energy boost
9 Storm ___
10 Treaters of dysphonia, for short
11 Drive
12 One who doesn't know how to get down?
13 Disobey an order?
14 Wagon, across the pond
18 Like a holiday acquaintance?
23 What capital letters may signify
24 Piece maker?
25 1982 film villain seeking to control the Genesis device
27 Sticky stuff
28 "The Stephen King of children's literature"
29 Drug that affects the heart rate
30 Request for one's word
32 Off-hand remark?
34 1994 movie in which the title character speaks an invented language
35 Major Adams of *Wagon Train*
37 Underwater insulation
40 Shell's shell, e.g.
41 Singer with the 1959 #1 hit "Why"
43 Reeling
45 "Thinking is the hardest work there is, which is the probable reason why ___ engage in it": Henry Ford
46 1, in Oaxaca
48 One of three in jai alai
49 Short move?
51 Religious title
52 Mini maker
53 ___ People's Democratic Republic

SET B

ACROSS

1 In uniform and ready to play
9 Harsh
15 Modern
16 Namesake of college football's Golden Arm Award
17 "Ask someone else"
19 They're run up the flagpole, figuratively
20 Little jerks
21 Abbr. on a food package, once
22 One of two states bordering eight others: Abbr.
23 Blueprint specification
25 Windsor, for one
26 Initial bit of progress
28 Cause to hang one's head
29 Scanner spec: Abbr.
31 Political figure nicknamed Young Hickory
32 Like algebraic symbols, often
33 Decrease?
35 17th-century philosopher who wrote *Ethics*
36 Follow
37 Make withdrawals over time?
38 In line with
39 State without really stating
40 Words after saying grace
42 Break new ground?
43 High-school clique
44 Metaphor for a headache
47 Peer Gynt's mother
48 Freaks (out)
49 Actor Novarro of 1925's *Ben-Hur*
50 Have multiple personalities?
54 "That sounds reasonable to me"
55 Song on *Beatles '65*
56 Proper
57 Half-court hoops game

DOWN

1 Command to a getaway driver
2 End of a poem by Horace
3 Start of an important announcement
4 Parmesan alternative
5 "Grand" brand
6 "Dear old" fellow
7 Pac-12 player
8 Bit of team motivation
9 Electrical problem
10 Sinusitis docs
11 Moxie
12 Upbeat sort
13 Leave to chance
14 Family vehicle, in Falmouth
18 Word sung at a New Year's Eve party
23 Far cry?
24 16-Across, e.g., for most of his career
25 1982 Ricardo Montalban role
27 Model builder's purchase
28 *Mostly Ghostly* series author
29 Foxglove
30 Start of a request for a guarantee
32 Bridge out?
34 Miss Fenwick of the Dudley Do-Right cartoons
35 "Really!?! with ___ and Amy" (*SNL* segment)
37 Surf shop rental
40 See 52-Down
41 Teen Angel portrayer in *Grease*, 1978
43 Euphoric
45 End of a Churchill quote about the Royal Air Force
46 When to celebrate the Festividad de San Sebastián
48 Multiplatinum Pink Floyd album, with "The"
49 Change places with a Realtor?
51 Comic actor DeLuise
52 Car company whose 40-Down includes a quartered circle
53 Vientiane native

ACROSS

1 Readied oneself
9 Extreme, as weather
15 Opposite of passé
16 Hall of Fame QB Johnny
17 "That falls under someone else's purview"
19 Notions
20 Harbor boats
21 Nutritional fig.
22 Part of TVA: Abbr.
23 Dieter's aid
25 Shoelace problem
26 Support for a mountaineer's foot
28 Disgrace
29 Meas. of inkjet printer resolution
31 President between Tyler and Taylor
32 Slanted, as type
33 Work through, as differences
35 Philosopher Baruch
36 Take the subsequent turn, as in a game
37 Gradually make less dependent
38 The "/" in "km/h"
39 Suggest
40 "Time to chow down!"
42 Cash register drawer
43 Third-century Germanic invaders
44 Workbench tool
47 Enzyme suffix
48 Barristers' wear
49 ___ Estévez (real name of Martin Sheen)
50 Have two outward identities
54 "You've convinced me"
55 Beatles song with the lyric "My tears are falling like rain from the sky"
56 In good taste
57 Basketball variation for four people

DOWN

1 "Hit the accelerator!"
2 Lyric poem
3 "Listen up!"
4 Ray of *Everybody Loves Raymond*
5 "Grand" ice cream brand
6 Father
7 4 x 4, for short
8 Words of encouragement before a game
9 Sudden onrush
10 Treelike residents of Middle-earth
11 Liveliness
12 Perpetually positive person
13 Completely mix up
14 Station wagon, to a Brit
18 "___ Lang Syne"
23 Scream
24 Filly's counterpart
25 Kublai ___
27 Strong glue
28 Goosebumps author R.L. ___
29 Cardiac stimulant derived from plant leaves
30 "I need verbal assurance from you . . ."
32 Nonbidder's declaration
34 *The Old Curiosity Shop* orphan
35 Brother of Cain and Abel
37 Diver's outfit
40 CBS's eye, e.g.
41 Burial place of King Arthur
43 Intoxicated with glee
45 *Never* ___ (1959 Sinatra film)
46 Febrero preceder
48 Mural's place
49 Move, in real estate lingo
51 ___ Pérignon
52 Mercedes competitor
53 Philosopher ___-tzu

IT COMES DOWN TO THIS by Merl Reagle

Featuring a lively collection of words devilishly clued.

SET A

ACROSS

1 Often adversarial advertiser
9 Like ABC or KLM
15 Warfare?
16 Big spoonful, say
17 Biblical book that tells the story of Bathsheba
18 It's often stuck in a corner
19 Mob target
20 Packing
22 Cinereous
23 Opposing force
25 Exclamation of exultation
27 Teen safety org.
28 Priest, at times
32 Miss at the Grand Ole Opry?
33 Agreeable comment
36 "Yeah, why not?!"
37 Cape Town to Durban dir.
38 One with anger management issues
40 Programming pros
42 Spanky wore one in *Our Gang* shorts
43 Meager
45 Calls up
46 Bit of text-message shorthand
47 Repeat offender
49 Girl in *The Last of the Mohicans*
51 Scholarship-offering org.
52 [That is so last year]
56 Guam is home to the world's largest one
58 Orsino's lover in *Twelfth Night*
61 "On each ___ the pea-hens dance": Yeats
62 Person of interest?
64 Cause of colonial unrest
66 1960s sitcom mother
67 Vituperate
68 Like the skies in "Don't Fence Me In"
69 Matching outfit

DOWN

1 Furniture trim
2 Husband of Bathsheba in 17-Across
3 Wallop
4 One of four rhyming letters
5 Poesia feature, often
6 Gush
7 Energy shortage
8 Author who died on the same day as John F. Kennedy and Aldous Huxley
9 They help keep people amused
10 "___ problem"
11 It has its orders
12 Top techie
13 Exercise program using a vertical bar
14 Conserve
21 Coffee shop order
24 The Atlas is the biggest one
26 Reason for shaking hands
29 Longtime TV Guide columnist Matt
30 53-Down competitor
31 A Chaucer pilgrim
33 Buck Owens song about a kiss with a mustache
34 Epiphany
35 Office distribution
39 Onetime Baryshnikov employer
41 Gender issue
44 *La Femme au Chapeau* artist
48 Foil
50 Heat
53 30-Down competitor
54 Follow-up to "yes"
55 Smart
57 Ariz. was one
59 Newswoman Logan
60 Like French's mustard, ironically: Abbr.
63 *War of the Worlds* weapon
65 Spray brand

SET B

ACROSS

1 Many an attack ad funder
9 Writ large?
15 Army food, once
16 Amount of cream, say
17 10th book of the Old Testament
18 Basic food item
19 Traitor
20 Partner of dangerous
22 Pale
23 1954 sci-fi film
25 Lucky lottery player's cry
27 Prom night safety org.
28 One who bestows with priestly authority
32 Hayride or hoedown participant
33 "Same here"
36 Deodorant brand
37 Last three letters of TNT
38 Very unjolly green giant
40 Workers at Black Rock, e.g.
42 Skye cap
43 Like some chances
45 Calls forth
46 "I think," in chat rooms
47 Persistent caller, perhaps
49 *The Postman Always Rings Twice* seductress
51 Driller's org.
52 [It's past my bedtime]
56 Former subsidiary of Sears
58 Oscar nominee Davis of *The Help*
61 Ewe milieu
62 Bank role
64 It prompted the slogan "No taxation without representation"
66 *Bewitched* character
67 Bawl out
68 Like the sky in a van Gogh painting
69 Dating dotcom

DOWN

1 Dodge
2 First name of an 'umble clerk
3 Edit menu command
4 Sweater letter
5 With "terza," a verse form
6 Rain cats and dogs
7 Weakness cause
8 *The Screwtape Letters* author
9 Picks out of a lineup, informally
10 Part of NB
11 Kind of act or action
12 One immersed in software development
13 Exercise program adapted from strip clubs
14 One way to reduce debt
21 Hole food?
24 Hole maker
26 Anxiety
29 Hall of Famer Edd
30 Kind of sign seen on a "4" key
31 *Somewhere in Time* star
33 Reaction to a wet willie, maybe
34 Occasion for a light bulb
35 Notes
39 ___ Ballet
41 Chromosome question
44 *Woman with a Hat* painter
48 Chivas Regal, e.g,
50 Zeal
53 Deadly compound?
54 "___ do better"
55 Cooper's ___ Bumppo
57 Guam, for one: Abbr.
59 Yuri's love in *Dr. Zhivago*
60 W. Hemisphere abbr.
63 One of the *Car Talk* guys
65 Tennis's Shriver

ACROSS

1 Fund-raising org. resulting from the Citizens United case
9 Using all uppercase letters
15 Army meal packs of WWII
16 Whipped cream amount
17 One of two Bible books named for a Hebrew judge and prophet
18 Paper clip alternative
19 Animal running a maze
20 Carrying a weapon
22 Pale-faced
23 Those people
25 Victor's shout
27 Unhappy-sounding but accident-deterring org. for teens
28 One who confers holy orders
32 Guy's partner
33 Playground response to "You are not!"
36 Positive
37 Opposite of WSW
38 "Incredible" comics hero
40 Network VIPs
42 Scot's cap
43 Slender
45 Brings to mind
46 "According to yours truly," in text message shorthand
47 One making unwanted advances
49 Mr. Dithers's wife in *Blondie*
51 Mil. program on campus
52 Sign of boredom
56 "Attention, ____ shoppers . . ."
58 Cousin of a cello
61 Pastoral setting, in poems
62 Bank, at times
64 1765 British move that outraged the Colonies
66 Mother-in-law on *Bewitched*
67 Go ballistic on
68 Like the night sky
69 Dotcom seeking compatible couples

DOWN

1 Mini, midi, or maxi
2 Dickens's ____ Heep
3 Stickum
4 Second letter after epsilon
5 Terza ____ (Italian verse form)
6 Serve, as wine
7 Iron-poor blood condition
8 Author of the Narnia books
9 Proof-of-age cards
10 "____ moment too soon!"
11 Roomful of students
12 Most technologically proficient person in a group, in slang
13 Strip club attraction
14 One obvious way to "save more"
21 Food with a hole
24 Pest attracted to light
26 Signal carriers in the body
29 Baseball Hall of Famer Edd
30 Four quarters
31 Man of Steel portrayer Christopher
33 Comment upon rubbing against a beard, maybe
34 Sudden insight
35 Interoffice notes
39 Russian ballet company
41 Chromosome choice
44 French painter Henri
48 ____ and soda
50 Passion
53 Where Bowie and Crockett made their last stand
54 The Beatles' "____ Work It Out"
55 Dapper, as a dresser
57 Yukon, for one: Abbr.
59 Tomb raider Croft
60 Made in the States: Abbr.
63 Bit of sunshine
65 Kitchen spray or girl's name

Fitting Words by Kevin G. Der

A wide-ranging 24-Across with some appropriately twisty clues.

SET A

ACROSS

1 Tipping point?
9 Activity involving three steps
15 Jesus Christ, with "the"
16 An untold amount
17 "Happy to!"
18 Circular, maybe
19 Food production movement since the 1970s
21 Animated monkey with a fez
22 Tiny circus attraction
23 Presses
24 [See blurb]
25 Pitch
26 Split
27 Ones bearing high interest?
31 San ___
32 Farthest point in an orbit around the moon
33 Target alternative
34 Crush
35 Envoys resolve them
36 "___ I?"
37 1801 discovery once classified as a planet
38 Good point of view?
39 Makes up for lost time, in a way
40 Where Phoebe performed, on *Friends*
44 Giver of the advice "Be sincere; be brief; be seated," in brief
45 Phrase accompanying a high-five
47 Bank, often
49 Think best
50 Put into gear?
51 Sparkling symbol
52 Theologian who gave his name to a Connecticut university
53 In person, often

DOWN

1 [How sad!]
2 M, for example
3 Complement of an orange
4 Largest suburb of Cleveland
5 One of TV's Mavericks
6 Challenge for one who's lost
7 Double-quick
8 Family units
9 Phone cords, typically
10 Go over the edge of?
11 Much skywriting
12 What an overwhelming favorite has
13 Apatosaurus, e.g., but not a tyrannosaurus
14 Kids in the 90s?
20 Sound unit
24 Symbol for a photon
25 ___ double
26 Rises
27 Hamartia
28 Subject of a hymn by Sappho
29 "Clear conscience" motto
30 Deserted
31 Set of reps?
33 Began digging
35 Pessimistic
37 Grand ___
39 1980s pop singer Hart
40 Sort that gets the red carpet treatment
41 Bud
42 Threw
43 Satan, with "the"
45 Historical setting
46 "___ is a bottomless cup; I will pour and pour": Euripides
48 Love

SET B

ACROSS

1 Cap part
9 Hip-swinging dance
15 Church of the ___
16 Too much to count
17 "Consider it done!"
18 Embed
19 Local, as cuisine
21 *Aladdin* monkey
22 Dog biter
23 Impels
24 [See blurb]
25 Long talk
26 Cut drastically, say
27 Nuts
31 One of the 12 tribes of Israel
32 Farthest point in an orbit around the moon
33 "Save money. Live better" sloganeer
34 Untold number
35 Some Chopin piano pieces
36 Fail to be, briefly
37 Largest body in the asteroid belt
38 Exclusive area
39 Makes final preparations?
40 Bistro
44 2012 Bill Murray political role, for short
45 "Way to go, partner!"
47 One maintaining a claim
49 Think very highly of
50 School rule subject
51 Diamond in Arkansas, e.g.
52 John who founded Methodism
53 Person who's rarely out?

DOWN

1 Act like a bloodhound
2 ___ passage
3 Like clear skies
4 Prosciutto di ___
5 Author ___ Easton Ellis
6 Gambler's goal, at times
7 Quickly
8 Domestic establishments
9 Mattress supporters
10 Improve
11 Web page distractions
12 What an undisputed frontrunner has
13 Grazing animal, e.g.
14 Upper-class kids?
20 Measure of acoustic intensity
24 Kind of ray
25 Hinder, as growth
26 Hollywood ___ (section of Los Angeles)
27 Key element in Greek tragedies
28 Contender for the Apple of Discord
29 "I wouldn't go back and change a thing"
30 How soloists perform
31 Group taking orders
33 Grew fond of
35 Ursine
37 Word on a magnum
39 Old-time comedian Professor Irwin ___
40 Red carpet walker, informally
41 Pal
42 Discombobulated
43 Adversary
45 Days of ___
46 Bad feeling?
48 Nothing at all

SET C

ACROSS

1 Adjustable fedora feature
9 Latin American dance with a shuffle
15 One from Jesus' hometown
16 Lots
17 "No problem for me!"
18 Sunday newspaper supplement
19 Local and fresh, as food
21 ___ Dhabi
22 Biting insect
23 Primitive impulses
24 [See blurb]
25 Pitch to a customer
26 Split down the middle
27 Diehard supporters
31 San ___ (Hearst castle site)
32 Farthest point in an orbit around the moon
33 Chain based in Bentonville, Ark.
34 Mob
35 Some French verses
36 Bing Crosby's "___ You Glad You're You?"
37 Roman goddess of agriculture
38 Pricey theater section
39 Studies at the last minute
40 ___ au lait
44 New Deal inits.
45 "Good job, dude!"
47 One holding a claim on property
49 View as perfect
50 Clothing
51 Florida's is moonstone
52 Retired general Clark
53 One who doesn't get out much

DOWN

1 Quick smell
2 Pronounced like "Mont Blanc"
3 Shade akin to sapphire
4 Italian city known for its cheese
5 Harte who wrote "The Outcasts of Poker Flat"
6 Winning back
7 Very quickly
8 Households
9 Snake shapes
10 Sharpen
11 TV spots
12 Big advantage in a race
13 Plant eater
14 Smart set
20 ___ canto
24 Beta follower
25 Walking on a high wire, e.g.
26 *Beverly ___ Cop*
27 Achilles' heel
28 Woody Allen's *Mighty ___*
29 "I wouldn't have done anything differently"
30 Unaccompanied
31 Group that often works on commission
33 Began to like
35 Fearing a drop in the stock market
37 Premier ___ (wine designation)
39 Actor Feldman
40 Star
41 Friend, south of the border
42 Stunned
43 Foe
45 Time long past
46 Feeling toward a 43-Down
48 Shutout score

SET A

ACROSS

1 It's hard to get a rise out of them
10 Defeat ignominiously
15 Sharp competition
16 Marina Piccola setting
17 Blocks in a bowl
18 Crack
19 Attendant on Cleopatra, in *Antony and Cleopatra*
20 Pulitzer-winning novel by Marilynne Robinson
22 Super Mario Bros. debuted on it
23 Stoked
24 Discombobulated
25 Pop flies?
26 Stripper's show
28 Sight from the blind
29 Soak
30 ___ *Woman* (Gary Cooper/Claudette Colbert film)
32 Promoted
34 Birthplace of poet/playwright Derek Walcott
38 Shot
39 Bowie colleague
41 Paradise of *On the Road*
42 Actuarial concern
43 Hardly a pickup artist
45 Ones with high aspirations?
49 Midwest city with a neighborhood called Campustown
50 Green cinches
52 Michaelmas mo.
53 "Phooey!"
54 Offer enticingly
55 Uniform
56 Bad at capitalization?
58 Makes the needle swing, maybe
60 Animal for un illusionniste
61 Novel on which the film *The Omega Man* was based
62 "Taste is the ___ of creativity": Picasso
63 Building for players

DOWN

1 Major joint
2 Mediterranean bay
3 Just slept in, perhaps
4 Memory problems
5 Biblical mount
6 Leaves base
7 Go around
8 Start a number with 9, maybe
9 Fifth element?
10 Large amount
11 Small amount
12 Drill command?
13 Dapper character on many cans
14 Times for retiring?
21 Hocks, essentially
24 Inseparable
25 Salt shakers
27 Ear covers
31 Originally, the sixth hour after dawn
33 One of Lemony Snicket's Baudelaire orphans
34 It might lead you to draw a blank
35 The 2010 America's Cup was won by one
36 Despair
37 Canaries' surroundings
40 Guinness Book's "most widely watched factual TV program in the world"
44 Renewal form checkbox
46 Institute whose teachers included Ken Kesey, Buckminster Fuller, and Ansel Adams
47 Prompt
48 Short suit, often
51 Hot downtown Manhattan nightclub of the late 1980s
54 "For He's a Jolly Good Fellow" verb
55 Saltimbocca seasoning
57 Title orphan who befriends Teshoo Lama
59 Wine designation

SET B

ACROSS

1 Lazy sorts
10 None-too-graceful dance
15 "Ideas for Life" sloganeer
16 Resort island in the Tyrrhenian Sea
17 Treat for Trigger
18 Expert
19 Plans for the future, briefly
20 Balm source
22 Wii ancestor
23 Janet Yellen's domain, with "the"
24 Flustered
25 Police jacket letters
26 Crayola color renamed "peach"
28 Get down from that!
29 One unlikely to pass the bar
30 Hellos
32 Put in a good word for
34 Island whose capital is Castries
38 Beanbag chair fill
39 Tubbs's partner on *Miami Vice*
41 Component of aqua marina
42 Game originally called La Conquête du Monde
43 Housekeeper's bane
45 Creatures of habit?
49 Leon of *Meet Me in St. Louis*
50 Simple strokes on the green
52 Third qtr. closer
53 Word appearing just twice in Dickens's *A Christmas Carol*
54 Are suspended
55 Matching
56 Opened in billiards
58 Fibs
60 Rabbit, to Rabelais
61 1954 Richard Matheson novel
62 Opposing group
63 Passage with increasing volume

DOWN

1 Doobie's brother
2 Wreath material
3 Destroyed
4 Spark plug features
5 Bonehead
6 Cradle support, in rhyme
7 Surround, poetically
8 Use an international code, maybe
9 Flask feature
10 Large quantity
11 Young boy
12 Dental directive
13 Planter's figure
14 Bathroom visits, euphemistically
21 Low joints
24 Stocky
25 Balloons
27 Does an oyster bar job
31 Day break?
33 One of the vampires on the CW's *The Originals*
34 Game originally called Criss-Crosswords
35 Multihulled yacht
36 Give up, in a way
37 Amazon outlet
40 BBC show that's a vehicle for vehicles
44 Alternative choice to "Payment enclosed"
46 California personal growth institute
47 Do a memo's job
48 Michael Phelps sponsor
51 Singers Rankin and Carter
54 Contradict
55 Word for the wise
57 Big name in North Korea
59 Wall St. watchdog

SET C

ACROSS

1 Late risers
10 Walk none too quietly
15 Brand of Japanese electronics
16 Blue Grotto setting
17 Cubes for coffee
18 Proficient
19 S&L offerings
20 Balm of ___ (fragrant resin)
22 Game console that debuted in Oct. 1985
23 Nourished
24 Pitched, as from a horse
25 Smack, as a fly
26 Skin
28 Avoid a beanball
29 Overindulger of the grape
30 Sue Grafton's ___ for Homicide
32 Hyped
34 Island south of Martinique
38 BBs, for example
39 Frontiersman Davy
41 Mineo of Giant
42 Jeopardize
43 Neatnik's opposite
45 Manipulative sorts
49 Home of Iowa State
50 Easy putts
52 Aug. follower
53 Scrooge utterance
54 Hang loosely
55 Identical
56 Bankrupt
58 Commits perjury
60 Rabbit fur
61 2007 Will Smith movie
62 Foe
63 Musical increase in loudness

DOWN

1 Large marijuana cigarette
2 Hardy's partner in comedy
3 Like beds before the housekeeper gets to them
4 Interstices
5 Donkey
6 Tree branch
7 Form a ring around, in poems
8 Make a call from a hotel, say
9 Soda bottle feature
10 Big amount
11 Smidgen
12 Request from a dentist
13 Commercial figure with a cane and monocle
14 Refueling opportunities at Daytona
21 Where bungee cords are attached
24 Thin's partner . . . and opposite
25 Bloats
27 "Aw, gee!"
31 Afternoon nap
33 Actor Kinski
34 Game played on a 15-by-15 grid
35 Boat with three side-by-side hulls
36 Become completely discouraged
37 Part of college sports' ACC
40 Car show on BBC America
44 Alternative to "Payment enclosed" on a renewal form
46 Big Sur's ___ Institute
47 Jog the memory of
48 Big name in little swimwear
51 Dickens girl and others
54 Say no to
55 Wise one
57 Novak of Vertigo
59 Part of a min.

The coveted ACPT Championship Bowl

Finalists at the playoff boards

2014 ACPT champion Dan Feyer

Round 5:
TOURNAMENT PLAY

This section is set up to match our 2014 tournament. If you'd like to find out how you would have finished if you had competed that year, using official ACPT scoring rules, follow these steps:

1. SOLVE THE PUZZLES.

Before you begin, set a timer so you do not exceed the time limits indicated for each puzzle:

- Puzzle #1 — 15 minutes
- Puzzle #2 — 25 minutes
- Puzzle #3 — 30 minutes
- Puzzle #4 — 20 minutes
- Puzzle #5 — 30 minutes
- Puzzle #6 — 30 minutes
- Puzzle #7 — 45 minutes

Ready? Go!

If you run out of time, stop. Your score is calculated on the amount of the puzzle that you finish within the time limit. Empty squares and incorrect letters count the same, so there is no penalty for guessing.

If you finish under the time limit, note your time for each puzzle. You get a bonus for each full minute under the time limit.

2. MARK YOUR CORRECT ANSWERS.

Turn to the answers on page 122, and mark your solutions.

3. SCORE YOURSELF.

Award 10 points for every correct answer Across and Down. For example, if a puzzle has 76 answers, you score 760 points for accuracy.

4. ADD YOUR TIME BONUS.

If you finish a puzzle before the time limit, award yourself 25 time bonus points for each full minute by which you finished early. For example, if a puzzle has a 15-minute time limit and you finished it perfectly in 11 minutes 45 seconds, you would score three minutes of time bonus, or 75 points (3 × 25).

Note, however: The time bonus is reduced by one minute for every incorrect or missing letter up to the point that the time bonus returns to zero. Thus, if you finished three minutes early but had two wrong letters, you would score one minute of time bonus, or 25 points. The time bonus cannot be negative, so if you missed more letters than the number of minutes you finished early, ignore the time bonus.

5. GET AN ACCURACY BONUS.

For each completely correct crossword, award yourself 150 accuracy bonus points.

6. ADD UP ALL YOUR POINTS FOR THE SEVEN PUZZLES.

Then turn to page 100–101 to discover your percentile ranking and how you match up against this tournament's competitors.

PUZZLE	TIME LIMIT	YOUR TIME	TOTAL ANSWERS	CORRECT ANSWERS	TIME BONUS	TOTAL SCORE
Puzzle #1	15 minutes		76 answers			
Puzzle #2	25 minutes		100 answers			
Puzzle #3	30 minutes		120 answers			
Puzzle #4	20 minutes		74 answers			
Puzzle #5	30 minutes		92 answers			
Puzzle #6	30 minutes		116 answers			
Puzzle #7	45 minutes		144 answers			

RANKINGS

ALL CONTESTANTS

The top score achieved at this tournament was 12,195 points.
You can estimate your percentile ranking here:

Score	Top		Score	Top
11,375	5%		8,495	55%
10,920	10%		8,290	60%
10,525	15%		7,940	65%
10,165	20%		7,630	70%
9,905	25%		7,345	75%
9,655	30%		7,095	80%
9,450	35%		6,510	85%
9,200	40%		5,925	90%
9,025	45%		4,730	95%
8,790	50%			

JUNIORS DIVISION (25 YEARS AND UNDER)

The top score achieved by
a junior was 11,925 points.

Score	Top
9,650	25%
8,375	50%
6,480	75%

FIFTIES DIVISION (50–59 YEARS)

The top score achieved by a 50s
contestant was 12,020 points.

Score	Top
10,300	25%
9,065	50%
7,735	75%

SIXTIES DIVISION (60–69 YEARS)

The top score achieved by a 60s contestant was 11,895 points.

Score	Top
9,385	25%
8,540	50%
7,320	75%

SENIORS DIVISION (70 YEARS AND OLDER)

The top score achieved by a senior was 11,400 points.

Score	Top
8,740	25%
7,645	50%
6,250	75%

ROOKIES DIVISION

The top score achieved by a rookie was 11,545 points.

Score	Top
8,615	25%
7,455	50%
6,000	75%

1. TO TELL THE TRUTH by Kelly Clark

Getting the tournament off to a no-nonsense start.

ACROSS

1 Nifty
5 Black card
10 Campus area
14 VFW sort
15 Like some charts in almanacs
16 Strongly recommend
17 Magic password, in a tale
19 Shortly
20 Soft drinks
21 Locales for bowl games
23 "My Way" singer
28 Like below-the-knee hemlines
31 Takes a stab
32 Grand Ole ___
33 Pester
38 Slate workers, for short
39 Porky's place
40 1979 Billy Joel song . . . or a hint to the starts of 17-, 23-, 49- and 62-Across
41 "Vive le ___!"
42 Help out
43 Otis who founded the Otis Elevator Co.
44 Sound from a bell tower
45 "That is to say . . ."
47 Like a 50th anniversary
49 Classic comic reality show
54 "Gracious!"
55 Op-ed piece, e.g.
59 Guinea pigs, maybe
62 Land and buildings
64 Gentleman caller, quaintly
65 "See ya"
66 School on the Thames
67 Spill (over)
68 Gallic girlfriends
69 Majority of blue staters

DOWN

1 Revivalists, informally
2 Montreal event of '67
3 Like centenarians
4 Noted Sarah Palin imitator
5 Sault ___ Marie, Mich.
6 Galileo, for one
7 "It was ___ and stormy night"
8 Hokey sign on a bathroom door
9 1983 Nicholas Gage memoir
10 Distant emitter of electromagnetic radiation
11 Vase
12 Long, long ___
13 Relative of a man cave
18 Lith. and Ukr., before the '90s
22 On edge
24 Playwright Fugard
25 Steering gear component
26 Like many homes on HGTV
27 Appoint, as to a task
28 Tiled artwork
29 Midsize Kia sedan
30 Poet called "Glorious John" by Walter Scott
34 *Wheel of Fortune* buy
35 Hi-___ graphics
36 ___ Wednesday
37 Oater transport
40 Sonja on ice
44 Gosh-darn
46 Makes sense
48 Mined substances
50 *The Little Rascals* girl
51 Saucerful for a cat
52 Cremona artisan
53 Fracas
56 Fill to the gills
57 Molecule part
58 Hankerings
59 The Cookie Monster's network
60 Sushi fish
61 Eastern path
63 Medical drama locales, for short

2. FIVE BOROUGH BRIDGES by Patrick Blindauer

Bringing all the parts of New York City together.

ACROSS

1 Time limit
7 "Zip-a-Dee-Doo-___"
10 Approach aggressively
16 Patriotic chant
17 ___ alai
18 "You got me!"
19 DC name since 1939 . . .
20 . . . Word with high or top . . .
21 . . . One behind the other
22 Hard Wasser
23 *Bus Stop* playwright
25 Mother of Horus
27 Parapsychology subj.
28 Snooty so-and-so
30 Fizz up
32 Sample
34 King James of the NBA . . .
36 . . . TV talent show imported from England, with "The"
38 Sweet pea, e.g.
41 One-eighth portion
43 Centipede runner
44 "Already?"
46 Wonderful feeling?
49 Lincoln player . . .
51 . . . Vital part: Var.
54 Some chart checkers: Abbr.
55 *Disraeli* Oscar winner George
57 Fictional character parodied in *The Princess Bride*
58 Where Mahmoud Ahmadinejad was once mayor
60 Parts of many choral formations
61 Slanted . . .
64 . . . Guarantee
67 Facetious features?
68 More slothlike
70 Sole means of support
74 Wile E. Coyote prop
75 PGA member?: Abbr.
77 Account for those with time to invest
79 ___ king
80 It may be passed on after a passing . . .
82 . . . ___ *for Noose* (Sue Grafton novel) . . .
84 . . . 1936 also-ran
86 Like some Sure things?
87 Princess of operetta
88 Minor mission
89 Contemptuous looks
90 Many a millennium
91 Old ___ (electric chair)

DOWN

1 8, 27, and 64, e.g.
2 Lightning Bolt
3 Joe's *Midnight Cowboy* buddy
4 Giant syllable?
5 Actor Morales
6 Poseur
7 Video game with a turntable
8 ___ Approved (sign)
9 "Let's rock!"
10 Nay-saying
11 Like beachfront property
12 Bengals, on a scoreboard
13 Most queer
14 Takes care of
15 Mess (with)
24 Like sauerkraut: Abbr.
26 Pleasure seekers' buys
29 Jacket writing
31 Years, abroad
33 Pro
35 Title related to "admiral"
37 Many a Laplander
38 Bert who was a Leo, fittingly
39 Old school

40 Hootenanny partners
42 Newspaper units: Abbr.
44 Brownish-orange horses
45 Where a famous R&H musical takes place
46 Loan figs.
47 Informant's under-wear?
48 Slaughter of St. Louis
50 The Gathering Place
52 Bygone autocrat
53 Prophet whose name means "salvation"
56 1966 hurricane between Hallie and Judith
58 Acapulco uncle
59 Almost 80% of it crosses water
60 Robs
61 *Wagon Master* and *The Westerner*
62 Robert Guillaume series
63 Minute
65 "Enjoy the ride" sloganeer
66 Last word of "America, the Beautiful"
69 Sharpshooter Oakley
71 Shower shower?
72 Loud, thudding sound
73 Good around the house
76 Cong. VIPs
78 50-and-over org.
81 Draft pick
83 "Yes"
85 PAC for packers?

3. SILENCE OF THE LAMPREYS by Merl Reagle

Beware the slippery clues!

ACROSS

1 Order (around)
5 Window part
9 Old geographical inits.
12 Fictional character with a white scar
16 Mince words, maybe?
17 "Too rich for my blood"
19 "I already ___"
20 Cousin of "voilà!"
21 Zero
22 Way to avoid kittens?
24 Insurance options, in brief
25 Fontana di ___
27 Type for titles: Abbr.
28 Debussy contemporary
30 Sister city of Thigh, New York?
35 Muse of comedy
36 NYSE watcher
37 They change a lot on *SNL*
39 Box office sign
40 Holder and others
43 Neighbor of Mary on TV
46 Bird sound
47 Where some download lawsuits are settled?
50 Sequel to *Das Boot*?
52 Semicircular recesses
53 Way of Paris
54 Lettuce-prep step
55 Ballpark buy
56 What goes between "Toys" and "Us" in a store sign?
59 Collette or Morrison
63 ___.com (info site)
65 Pulp fiction piece?
66 RBI king
67 Q: "So, Tarzan, does actor Gosling rent his tuxedos?" A: "No, ___."
70 Saw a one-named rock star in concert?
73 My relative?
74 Fastidious TV figure
76 Gets in return
77 "Hmm, never thought of that!"
78 TV money maven
80 Do a yard job
82 Tad
84 All 11 members of a football team?
89 Dream: Prefix
90 Tight feeling
91 Neck protector
94 Put in folders
96 What's out of a hoopster's hands?
100 Eclectic mix
101 Assemble-it-yourself brand
102 Mendes of movies
103 Simmons alternative
104 Traditional, quaintly
105 Gershwin heroine
106 "Done ___?"
107 Covers
108 Strong cleaners

DOWN

1 Natural talent
2 Polecat's defense
3 Billionaire publisher of *Vogue* and *Vanity Fair*
4 Sugar substitute
5 Creamy or extra crunchy brand
6 French Facebook contact
7 Pluck
8 Ashtray fill
9 Chess ploy, briefly
10 "Photograph" singer
11 Change the price of, say
12 Watcher over Odysseus
13 Composer Marvin
14 Commotion
15 First degrees, for short
18 Problem word for Porky
23 "___ Have Left the Building" (alternate title for this puzzle)
26 Mooring spots
29 Parish priests
31 Lead-in to copter: Var.
32 Oliver Twist, for one
33 I, in Innsbruck
34 Yours, to Yves
35 Figure of speech
38 Soak (up)
39 Line crosser
41 Proofing mark
42 Thing with a rowel
44 Asgard's ruler
45 Mao's successor
48 Printed again
49 Stone city of Jordan
51 Assailed
54 Mountain feature
56 Square setting
57 Like Christmas stockings
58 50 minutes, notoriously, for a therapist
60 At first
61 Three-trio combo
62 *Picnic* Pulitzer winner
64 Post-convention polling effect
66 Liquid or frozen items
67 Pal of Pooh
68 Mongolian tent
69 Vest features
70 Pond sounds
71 *Death Becomes Her* costar
72 "Decorated" as a prank
75 911 respondent
79 Queen Dido's lover
81 Drinks on a list
83 Chill
85 Dance troupe founder
86 Show to be true
87 Prize founder
88 Provider of Steve Jobs's first job
92 Ferris wheel, e.g.
93 Them, to us
94 Short story?
95 '50s campaign nickname
97 Muesli ingredient
98 Classic Ford
99 Part of UNLV

4. SPACED OUT by MaryEllen Uthlaut

An invasion of otherworldly puns.

TIME LIMIT	YOUR TIME	CORRECT ANSWER
20 MINUTES		

ACROSS

1. Palindromic title
6. Puts in a part
11. Unrefined
14. Ambience enhancer
15. Mother to Barbara and Jenna
16. Letter found in the letters before and after it
17. 37-Across who's inexperienced?
19. Put a strain on
20. Loyal subject
21. Capital on the Missouri
23. The consonants "p," "v," "m" and "w," in phonetics
26. Hearty steak
27. Intertwine
28. "My, my!"
29. Collected quotes
30. Small drum
32. Packs in a knapsack, say
35. Acne memento
37. One who's not from around here
39. "Sweetest nymph," to Milton
40. Young 'uns
42. Party mixer
44. Keystone officer
45. Long vowel indicator
47. Grapefruit-like fruit
49. Wraps in cloth
51. Old Faithful, e.g.
52. Man, woman, or child
53. Gestational units
54. Sherwood Forest shelter
55. 37-Across waiting for some boats to come in?
60. The Beatles' "All ___ Got to Do"
61. Fulcrum bar
62. Indigenous plants
63. Serve to do over
64. Doesn't take a hit, in blackjack
65. Fake

DOWN

1. *S.I.* or *W*
2. Music sheet: Abbr.
3. Unidentified John
4. 2009 Hilary Swank title role as an aviatrix
5. Crazies
6. Drano targets
7. Rhine tributary
8. Bask at the beach
9. Fearful
10. *Don Quixote* and *The Simpsons*
11. 37-Across who digs classic '60s music?
12. Maker of Pong
13. Candlelike
18. Capital near the Missouri
22. Make happy
23. Cleared a hurdle, say
24. Get to
25. 37-Across with a demerit?
26. What lacquer leaves
28. The Hunter
31. Cher and others, voicewise
33. Unabridged
34. Narcoleptic state
36. Poet with the epitaph "Here lies One Whose Name was writ in Water"
38. Bit a bit
41. Smith and Brown
43. Food Network event
46. Milk curdler
48. Biceps, e.g.
49. Go bad
50. Hair extensions
51. Ones for whom life is predictable?
53. Curds' partner
56. Federal energy corp.
57. Ornamental fish
58. Unit of work
59. Black and ___ (pub drink)

5. SEND IN THE CLONES by Brendan Emmett Quigley

Watch out for some double-crossers! They may sneak in when you're not looking.

ACROSS

1 Viracocha worshiper
5 It can get under your skin
11 Raw ___
16 Join
17 Multimeter measurement
18 Spoken in French?
19 Stabs / Some lodgings
21 Toast
22 Constellation next to Triangulum Australe
23 Jean Eugène Robert-___, the Father of Modern Magic
24 Ted who created *The Three Stooges*
25 General ___
27 Caught
28 Metaphor for life
29 Succeed
30 Anderson who directed *The Grand Budapest Hotel*
31 "Soup's on!"
34 Bug exterminator?
36 Meets
37 Grp. with 17 classes
40 Stretch out
43 Soft's opposite
44 Physical response?
45 Crane's location / African tourist destination
47 Stick game
48 Leveler
50 Pirate known for charity
51 Man's man?
52 Silver dollars, maybe
54 Designer Kenneth
56 Patient scene
57 *The Daughter of Time* author Josephine
59 Message board?
63 Beer feature
64 Foot: Lat.
65 Apache warriors?
66 Laid-back, in slang
68 Southern college town
70 Guitar part
71 "Is this thing on?"
72 Tried / 1964 title role
74 "Ding-Dong! The Witch Is Dead" composer
75 Cry with a bell
76 Not really a friend
77 Evening aid
78 One to catch up with at a reunion
79 Snafu

DOWN

1 "Sounds good"
2 Signal relayer
3 Slipper's need?
4 Pitches
5 Pacific salmon
6 What came before you?
7 Bad mark
8 Some keyboards
9 Tour organizer
10 Old gaming inits.
11 Results
12 Pretend to be
13 *Richard III* costar / Fattening?
14 Employer of many screeners
15 Bank
20 Detention time, maybe
26 Comatose
28 Has as a tenant
30 Like fingerprints
31 Limpidness
32 Chambers in a chest
33 Double-platinum double album of 1969
35 Mental
36 Bring (in)
37 Fairyflies, e.g.
38 Religion whose symbol is a nine-pointed star
39 Something "fine" at a dinner party / Stole stuff, maybe
41 "Los ___ cerditos" (Spanish children's story)
42 Shofar source
46 ___ d'Argenteuil, celebrated French nun
49 *Richard III* costar
53 Popular shellfish
55 USD alternative
57 Multiple-choice answers, often
58 F, to the ear
60 Dictate
61 Stereotypical butler
62 Puts out
64 *Slumdog Millionaire* star
65 Religious figure
66 Break in the winter
67 Heave
69 One-named Grammy winner
72 Cable channel, in TV listings
73 Half of an old radio comedy team

6. UH . . . LIKE . . . YOU KNOW? by Anna Shechtman

He who hesitates is not lost!

ACROSS

1 "Sis boom bah" preceder
7 Alternative to "To whom it may concern"
15 "What's cookin'?"
18 Ring combination
19 Flashy two-pointer
20 Tax pro, briefly
21 What spilling the beans might accelerate?
23 Charged particle
24 "He shall suck the poison of ___": Job 20:16
25 Unlocks
26 Happening
28 PhD requirement: Abbr.
29 Fibrous muffin ingredient
33 Facebook or OkCupid creation
37 One singing psalms loudly?
41 Wives of rajahs
42 Features of some car deals
44 Disney's ___ & Stitch
45 Ultimatum's end
47 Destination for Paris tourists
48 One of the girls on Girls
49 Aid for psychics?
51 Alternative to baking?
54 False gods
55 Long-armed ape, informally
56 Spending according to plan
59 What a waiter does to supplement a main course?
64 Like Odin and Thor
65 Diva's solo
66 Spring times
67 "While you're ___ . . ."
68 Heavy metal or emo
72 "___ River" (song from Show Boat)
73 The Met, the Guggenheim, the Cooper-Hewitt, and six others that famously make up a New York "mile"?
75 Scrumptious bits
77 "Pineapple"
78 Mailed
79 Mrs. Gorbachev
81 Lauder of cosmetics
83 Emphatic response to "Quieres más?"
87 "We have ___ in order not to die of the truth": Nietzsche
88 Editors Harold Ross, William Shawn, and David Remnick?
94 Introduction to liberalism?
95 Pass at the plate?
96 Beginning
97 Sex columnist Savage
98 Source of extracts found in many beauty products
99 Mojave or Gobi

DOWN

1 Italia's capital
2 Enero-to-diciembre periods
3 Marijuana plant
4 US 1 and others: Abbr.
5 Part of a wheat stalk
6 Fondue bourguignonne potful
7 Julie Andrews and Judi Dench
8 Tesla CEO ___ Musk
9 Gov. Landon and others
10 No longer working: Abbr.
11 Assad's land: Abbr.
12 Debtor's promise
13 Hooey
14 Range of influence
15 Marie or Pierre Curie
16 "When You Wish ___ a Star"
17 Be winded
22 Unexpected win
27 Ones famous for overusing the words "like" and "totally"
28 Deter through argument
29 Do as one's told
30 Boxer with a 2-1 record against Frazier
31 Age at which Tatum O'Neal won an Oscar
32 Kids' ammo
33 Climactic scene in Carrie
34 In ___ form
35 Linear, in brief
36 Senate obstructions
37 Roseanne formerly of Roseanne
38 At a red light, say
39 Princess in Frozen
40 Horse of a certain color
43 Frequently bleeped Comedy Central presentation
46 Slate or Salon
48 Backpack brand
50 Cavs, on a scoreboard
51 Up to now
52 Supposed lead-in?
53 "Ta-___ Boom-de-ay!"
56 "___ unrelated note . . ."
57 "Don't look at me!"
58 Fighting words
59 Utah city
60 Halves of sawbucks
61 Attractive girl, in modern lingo
62 Alternative to Israir
63 Identification figs.
65 Fever and chills
68 Baltimore paper, with "The"
69 Main Street, ___
70 Breakfast spot, on special occasions
71 Arab commander: Var.
74 Say with sincerity
76 Monotheist's belief
78 British guns
79 Kentucky senator Paul
80 Zone
81 Deco illustrator
82 ___-Ball (arcade game)
83 Je ne ___ quoi
84 Playwright William
85 What not to do with 007's martini
86 "___ it a pity?"
89 Night before
90 "Aren't ___ pair?"
91 Up to now
92 Stroke implement
93 Choler

TIME LIMIT	YOUR TIME	CORRECT ANSWER
30 MINUTES		

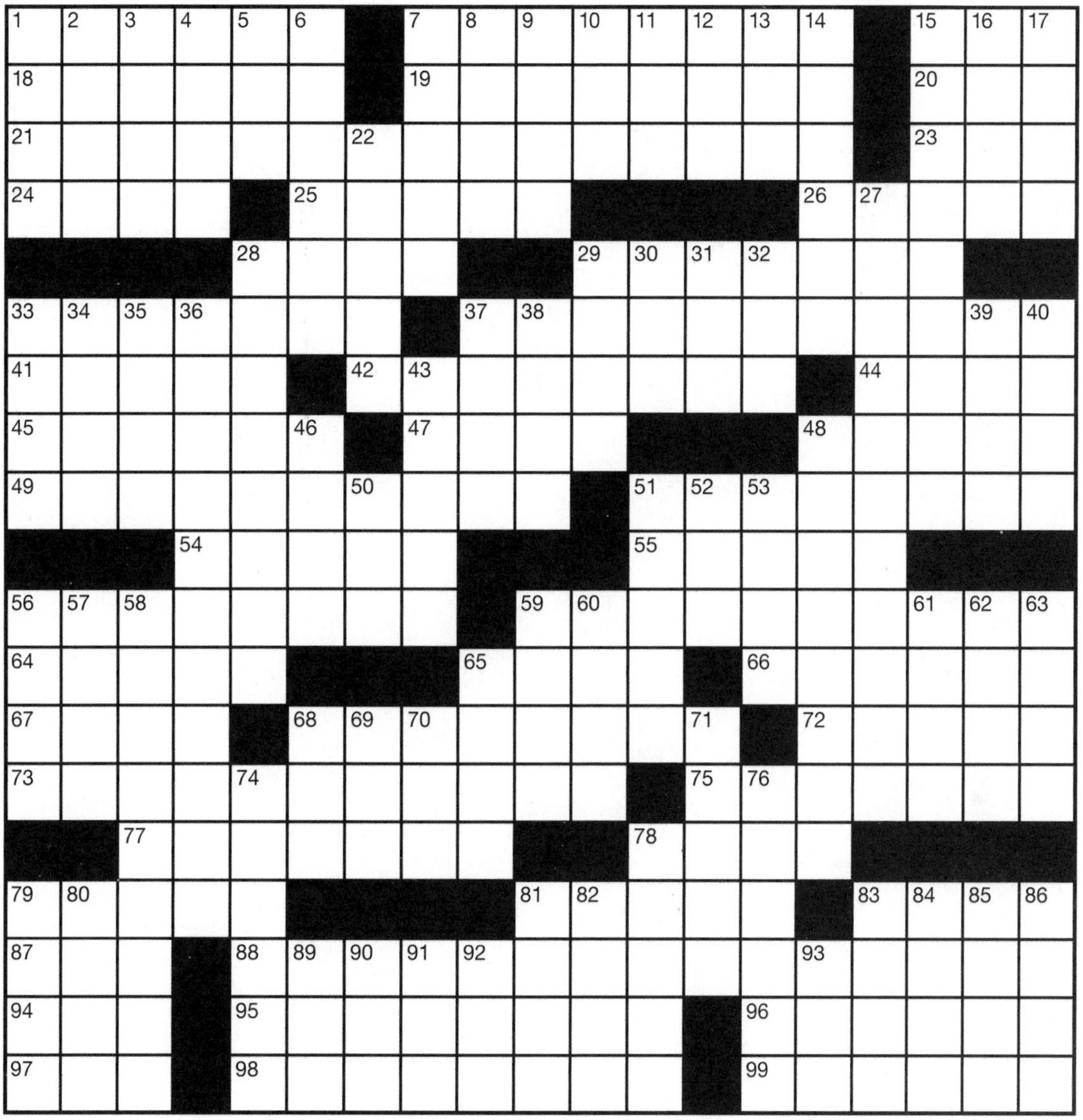

7. IT ALL ADDS UP by David J. Kahn

To complete this puzzle you'll need to think inside the box.

ACROSS

1 Carryall for some carriers
8 Interfere (with)
12 Suffix with drunk or dull
15 Clean Air Act target
19 Waldorf extension?
20 ___ sax
21 What a live broadcast is in
23 With 27-, 110- and 124-Across, clue to completing the center box of this puzzle's grid
25 Lunatic
26 Star next to Venus?
27 See 23-Across
29 Laptop key
31 Uneasy state to be in
32 Pep
36 Helmets, e.g.
41 Susie of *Curb Your Enthusiasm*
46 Noodle-based cuisine
47 1970s Chrysler compact
49 Sound
50 Graffiti artist
52 Time's partner, informally
53 Two-timer
56 Bush press secretary Fleischer
57 Garishly colored
60 Waterman, e.g.
61 Backyard storage space
62 WWII enlistee
63 Budget chain for travelers
65 Base runners at the corners, say
66 Pesky parasite
67 Staffer: Abbr.
69 Place for a lead story
70 Like some golf courses
72 Magnifies, with "up"
75 Paris's ___ d'Orsay
77 When to have dinner in a 1933 George Cukor film
78 Great movie rating
80 Like, in recipes
81 Ghostly visitors
84 Diamonds
87 Outback runners
88 Scotland's longest river
89 Hyundai compact
90 Tampa Bay team
92 Purchased rather recently, say
94 Piddling
95 Band leaders?

100 Top
101 Like a poli sci major, perhaps
104 Use a sailboard
105 Time piece?
106 Instructions to a boxer
108 One side of the Bering Strait
110 See 23-Across
118 Bring (up) from the past
123 What gets a good licking?
124 See 23-Across
126 Environmentalists' excursions
127 "Leave it"
128 Unborn
129 Staffs
130 Poet's contraction
131 Big cheese
132 Alternatives to bows

DOWN

1 Yoga class equipment
2 US Open's ___ Stadium
3 Roman way
4 Kind of wolf
5 Setting for mimosas
6 Get a bead on
7 Jabber
8 Albert behind a mike
9 "What ___ can go wrong?"
10 Move a little
11 Company behind *Jeopardy!*
12 Standing closet
13 Empire
14 It runs through four national capitals
15 Marvel-ous Lee
16 Material in sheets
17 Country on the Strait of Hormuz
18 Neuter
22 Cars with bars
24 Went looking for lampreys
28 Thunder sound
30 Fraternity character
32 Senators' place
33 *Gone with the Wind* family
34 When completed, this puzzle's center box, e.g.
35 Chauvinist
37 Rep.
38 Toss
39 World Series climax
40 Spinoff channel for armchair athletes

42 Soft drink named after a California volcano
43 Field of 34-Downs
44 Nautical direction
45 Unlikely prom king
47 Looking more disheartened
48 Staff sgt., e.g.
51 ___ leaf beetle
54 "Big flies," in baseball
55 *The Book of* ___
58 Actress Hagen
59 *Place de la Concorde* artist
61 Govt. security
64 Not forbid
65 Sounds of sympathy
68 Mole's work
71 Quick flight
73 ___ TV
74 Willie Mays catchphrase
76 Long-distance letters
79 Reno-to-LA dir.
81 Fiber source
82 Tiger or Twin, informally
83 Farm butter?
84 Golf club that produces a high loft
85 ___ monte
86 One looking through specs?
91 VW forerunner?
93 Isn't any longer
96 Hardly feeling reverential
97 Iwo ___
98 Fisherman's drag
99 Affable duo?
102 *Marco Polo Sings* ___ (John Guare play)
103 Emerge victorious
105 Good talking-to
107 Kind of pants
109 Menzel who won a Tony for *Wicked*
110 Consider
111 Victim of Pizarro
112 Classic name in paperbacks
113 Realizes
114 Crash-investigating org.
115 Inflict on
116 Motorcade paths: Abbr.
117 Horse course?
119 Rebuke to Brutus
120 Insect repellent
121 *Arbitrage* actor, 2012
122 Genesis grandson
125 Hi-___

BLACK AND WHITE

```
SAMBA CAFE  SPEW
ALIAS OBIT  YEAH
LISPS VERYANGRY
TEETERED MIO
    RITE  HARDJOB
MAYS  COHO  ISOLA
ALIT  OREGON  HMS
STN  YINYANG  NES
CID  ELAYNE  ANCE
OMEGA  TASS  SYST
TAXFREE    EATA
    OLD  NOCHANCE
EVERYINCH  EIGER
TALC  TEAM  ARENA
ACME  STAY  DELTS
```

ENCOURAGING WORDS

```
OMARS  SCAR  ALIA
NONET  ERIE  NODS
CONGRATULATIONS
ESAU  IUD  LEMMON
    LUMP  RITA
  SCARE  MAZELTOV
CHARGE  ICE  ELI
HORSE  INK  AGREE
ONO  MAC  TERROR
WELLDONE  AREAS
    IOUS  SHOE
ACESIT  SAO  NEAP
DONTTHATBEATALL
ALOE  ELAL  PESTO
YAWN  DIRE  EATAT
```

ARMS RACE

```
OBAMA  BANDS  DOH
LUNAR  AFOUL  ERA
ENNUI  GAMMA  JAN
 GOINGGREATGUNS
CAT  GAY    SERGE
ALAS  SPECS  TEEN
VOTER  ALAMOS
SWEATINGBULLETS
    LENTIL  DORIA
MICA  ASNER  WREN
INANE  MOI  ADD
SUREASSHOOTING
URN  RAPID  IDTAG
SEE  TRADE  NORMA
ESS  HAREM  ASYET
```

FLIP-FLOPS

```
COASTS  SPCA  MSG
UPSHOT  LSAT  EPA
SAYYOUSAYME  ZIP
SLEET  ENCE  ZEE
    SOMETHINGOLD
TOMTOM    NOR
AMA  YMCA  SAHIB
MAYBEYESMAYBENO
PROAM  LAPD  RTS
    KIT  EDSELS
SOMETHINGNEW
QUO  ESAU  JAMBS
UNO  DAYINDAYOUT
ACE  DUEL  AVERSE
TED  TKTS  RUDEST
```

BLITHE SPIRIT

```
TAEBO  CAPRI  JOB
OLDER  PCLAB  ORE
GAYMARRIAGE  LAD
ONSITE  DIG  ILLS
    NOHO  TESTY
NUMERALS  DWARFS
OSE  SSGTS  FLOAT
SURE  HAPPY  OGLE
EARLY  SARIS  ESE
ELYSEE  TEETERED
    WEANS  ELAL
AMIS  SAE  DMITRI
LED  SUNNYSIDEUP
PRO  SETTO  NENES
SEW  TSARS  ASTRO
```

PLUS TEN

```
JABS  PABLO  ATOP
EURO  CARET  NERO
TGIF  SAINTANNEX
AUDIS  BOOBOO
GREATAPEX  LURED
ESS  ESA  SENSED
    WALLACH  CAKE
  COMEINLATEX
ODOR  ENGINES
SENDUP  MIA  BYE
SATIN  CREAMALEX
  ENTIRE  SLUSH
CAMEOROLEX  IRMA
OOPS  ANISE  ARAL
BLTS  SECTS  SYNE
```

BUZZ WORDS

```
INEPT  ASSN  PAST
COLOR  BAKE  IRMA
ENGLISHLIT  TRIP
SURE  TOE  SCADS
UKE  BERMUDAHIGH
PECKAT  REX  GEO
  SOIL  WAGE  ANNE
    TIGHTENDS
ROME  OAFS  REFS
ONE  SAM  HEAROF
BASESLOADED  ITE
ETHAN  FUR  ASHE
ROUT  FIREBOMBED
TOGA  IDOL  DEERE
STAT  BOSS  SNEER
```

MAKING A LIST

```
BIDE  SHOP  ACTAS
AMEX  IOWA  WHITE
MASTODONS  AORTA
ACCRUED  SERPENT
    ASK  AGNES
  CASTINTODOUBT
FAR  SCOT  FERAL
OPUS  KMART  YALE
REBUS  BARK  VOX
SANTODOMINGAN
    DIARY  BEA
ALFALFA  BULLITT
MEANT  FAINTODOR
ONICE  TALE  RIDE
SOLED  YAKS  EGOS
```

CAN YOU DIG IT?

```
ELSE  HEAT  WHOMP
CELL  ARCH  ROMEO
OVAL  NILE  IMAGE
LIVINGQUARTERS
    OAS    ITEM
  CUTTINGREMARKS
ALB  ENTR  SEDONA
BOOM  HAM  EGAD
UNLESS  SOIE  EVE
GETSTHEPICTURE
    SEEM  EUR
  LIKESINABIGWAY
CAVIL  NOSE  EASE
AMATI  ETTE  ONKP
DENSE  MEIR  NESS
```

TWICE AS NICE

P	A	R	T	■	L	O	F	T	■	S	H	A	K	E
R	U	E	R	■	E	L	I	A	■	E	E	L	E	D
E	D	G	E	D	E	D	G	E	D	S	W	O	R	D
S	I	A	M	E	S	E	■	B	E	A	N	E	R	Y
S	O	L	O	S	■	■	R	O	A	M	■	■	■	■
■	■	■	R	I	N	S	E	■	R	E	D	E	E	M
I	K	E	■	R	O	U	S	E	■	■	E	L	M	O
D	E	C	K	E	R	D	E	C	K	E	R	B	U	S
E	G	G	O	■	S	A	T	I	N	■	A	S	H	■
A	S	S	I	G	N	■	T	O	N	I	S	■	■	■
■	■	■	O	O	H	S	■	■	G	I	B	B	S	■
O	V	E	R	A	T	E	■	S	U	M	M	E	R	Y
W	I	D	E	W	I	D	E	T	R	A	I	L	E	R
A	B	N	E	R	■	D	E	A	N	■	A	L	A	I
R	E	A	D	Y	■	A	N	T	S	■	N	A	D	A

WITHOUT FAIL

S	A	C	K	■	C	L	I	P	■	B	I	D	E	S
Q	U	A	Y	■	A	O	N	E	■	E	N	O	C	H
U	N	C	L	E	B	U	C	K	■	S	P	I	R	O
A	T	H	E	N	A	■	■	E	A	T	E	N	U	P
B	Y	E	■	U	N	A	■	D	A	N	G	■	■	■
■	■	■	B	R	A	S	S	H	A	T	■	T	O	E
Z	O	W	I	E	■	S	T	E	M	■	J	I	N	X
A	M	A	T	■	F	I	O	N	A	■	E	M	I	T
G	I	V	E	■	A	S	I	N	■	T	E	E	N	S
S	T	Y	■	J	U	I	C	E	B	A	R	■	■	■
■	G	M	A	N	■	■	R	O	C	■	A	D	E	■
H	E	R	E	I	A	M	■	■	W	I	G	O	U	T
E	M	A	L	L	■	B	L	O	W	T	O	R	C	H
L	E	V	E	E	■	A	U	T	O	■	O	T	T	O
D	R	Y	E	R	■	S	C	O	W	■	P	A	S	S

A UN ASSEMBLY

S	P	I	C	E	■	B	O	M	B	E	■	F	E	B
A	L	O	H	A	■	O	N	T	A	P	■	U	R	L
P	O	W	E	R	L	A	U	N	C	H	■	T	I	A
S	P	A	R	■	Y	R	S	■	C	R	O	U	C	H
■	■	■	U	A	R	■	■	H	H	O	U	R	■	■
■	R	A	B	B	I	T	H	A	U	N	T	I	N	G
M	E	N	■	O	C	E	A	N	S	■	I	S	E	E
E	N	D	T	O	■	A	D	D	■	M	E	T	A	L
S	T	Y	E	■	T	R	O	U	P	E	■	I	T	S
H	A	W	A	I	I	A	N	P	A	U	N	C	H	■
■	■	■	A	S	S	E	T	■	■	G	P	O	■	■
S	P	R	E	A	D	■	A	H	A	■	T	S	P	S
H	U	H	■	Y	O	U	R	E	N	O	F	A	U	N
A	M	O	■	S	W	A	I	N	■	F	O	R	T	E
G	A	L	■	O	N	E	L	S	■	T	R	I	T	E

TWO FOR THE SHOW

V	O	L	T	■	G	E	A	R	■	S	A	G	A	S
E	M	I	R	■	A	X	L	E	■	E	X	I	L	E
L	A	M	A	■	S	P	I	N	■	R	O	L	E	X
C	H	I	C	A	G	O	S	E	V	E	N	■	■	■
R	A	T	E	D	R	■	T	W	I	N	■	O	J	S
O	N	S	■	L	I	D	■	S	P	E	E	D	U	P
■	■	■	G	I	L	D	A	■	■	M	O	N	A	■
■	D	O	U	B	L	E	F	E	A	T	U	R	E	■
M	A	R	S	■	■	T	Y	R	O	S	■	■	■	■
B	I	G	H	A	I	R	■	E	T	D	■	A	T	L
A	S	S	■	B	R	I	E	■	S	O	T	R	U	E
■	■	■	T	R	A	F	F	I	C	S	I	G	N	S
J	U	L	I	O	■	L	I	T	E	■	N	Y	E	T
A	R	O	M	A	■	E	L	A	N	■	E	L	I	A
M	I	X	E	D	■	D	E	L	E	■	S	E	N	T

IMMORTAL COMBAT

(W)	A	C	O	■	H	E	(A)	D	■	S	P	A	(R)	
O	N	O	R	■	A	L	L	I	N	■	T	E	M	A
O	G	R	E	■	C	A	M	E	O	■	I	A	M	S
F	L	O	O	D	I	N	S	U	R	A	N	C	E	■
E	E	N	■	W	E	D	■	S	I	G	H	T	S	■
R	E	A	G	A	N	■	G	A	E	L	■	P	E	I
■	■	O	R	D	E	R	S	■	■	S	I	R	S	■
■	W	E	L	F	A	R	E	S	T	A	T	E	S	■
D	O	D	D	■	L	E	N	A	P	E	■	■	■	■
U	R	N	■	T	R	E	K	■	K	I	M	O	N	O
I	D	O	T	O	O	■	A	E	S	■	H	O	U	■
■	G	R	A	M	M	A	R	S	C	H	O	O	L	S
B	A	T	H	■	A	R	E	N	A	■	W	H	I	T
O	M	O	O	■	N	A	D	E	R	■	N	O	T	E
(G)	E	N	E	■	■	B	(O)	R	E	■	S	H	A	(D)

WHAT ARE THEY?

```
AFB  TREF ROTS PHEN
RELO HERE EROO ROPE
GRAYBEARD MAYFLOWER
UNCLAD EURO STALLED
ESK WOODPILE EVA
BOLTS ADAMSAPPLE
IMIN LAWS SOT SLID
NORTHPOLE GED HEAVE
FEDORA IAGO EKE YEN
POUNDSTERLING
UHF SLO ESTE DRAPES
HALAS OWL HARDYBOYS
OVEN SSE NEMO OWEN
HEADCHEESE THANE
ERA DAVISCUP RET
OFFRAMP FAME RABBLE
FROSTBITE BALLROOMS
MATE LUST ELIE GAEL
ETON ESPY DYED TRA
```

ELMER FUDDISMS

```
ABRADE SHAM SNOWS
DIESEL IOLA ANNOYED
SOCIAL THINASAWHALE
EDDA CUM TSK STEP
LEPEW WOMBMATES TSP
OAT IDEM ADD IFS
DROWNED OBI ANTIQUE
ENRAGE STALK AUBURN
DEMONIC IAN AGO
UNDER WICKETS HADES
RAU ALP BREAKUP
ASTRAL SPATS NEEDLE
LACONIA AYE READIER
HOE NAG TEEN SAL
ABT WOKBOTTOM DRONE
MAWR ILO OUT SKEW
THEIDLEWITCH EWINGS
STEVIES CAKE TAGEND
STEER ELSE HINDUS
```

SWITCHEROO

```
BABY MTAPO STEP HAJ
AURA EATUP ROMA ASU
STOWTHRONESAWAY NED
SONNETS INE SICKDAY
XENA EINE LUIS
NACRE NERDSBESTSOUP
ETH TROD EAR SANE
HOES UTICA YARD POW
IPECAC CABS TIOS
ROCKETFULLOFPIE
THUS ESAI LYNXES
FOP ESSO EMCEE ECRU
ABUT EVE ILSA LIE
DINOFINEQUITY BOUND
ITIN NUNS GATS
RISOTTO AIR CASTING
ACH FOURLOAFCLEAVER
JOE UNTO NERVE WEAR
AND LEST SLAIN ASPS
```

MISFILINGS

```
MET MSG PAST OMOO
ECHO NITA ONTO IOWA
ORES ODOR STAT LEEK
WUTHERINGHEIGHTS
SEEST ELO YEA AFT
MATH JELLO PABLO
RAP ASTUDYINSCARLET
UKES ENG THEE REDO
DISHRAG THEROBE
ENTRE SNEER ASTRO
IVANHOE MATTHAU
ACHE BIAS IAM SETS
LOOKBACKINANGER GET
BASSO ORALS RENO
AXE SAC ICC IDOLS
SCHOOLFORSCANDAL
DOZE EMMA VITA OBOE
OVER ABET EBON SUNG
NANA DONE SEW GEO
```

FUTURE WORLD

```
GAZEBO BLAST CREATE
AMORAL ROUTE HELPER
RONALDRAYGUN ALLOTS
BRET MUG TUNES
PEN VEE RCA GAD
SENDINTHECLONES ALA
CLOUT SONOMA EDGAR
ABIE PENATES EAST
LOSTVERIZON REAM
EWE APES ROAR SAO
SLID METEORMAIDS
SHOO CARAMEL SDAK
MIXUP ERASES THETA
IKE LEAVEITTOBIEBER
TEN ALP SLY LES
ENATE AAR AGED
INSTEP ROBOTREDFORD
COUNTS INANE TERESA
CREASE ESTEE SPORTY
```

FOODIE FILM FESTIVAL

```
GLORY ADD ATMS LIP
MINEO ROAR RHEA ASH
ALEEKOFTHEIROWN MLI
SVEN WEAR OPAL
GRUELINTERRUPTED
RIG TIARA IEOH
APART CREPESOFWRATH
FAREHIKES MEIF ROO
PRO BITS IRENE
SILENCEOFTHECLAMS
KANYE HANA BID
IST GURU YOUSAIDIT
THEKINGSPEACH DIEGO
LOCA BRAUN LOW
PUTTINONTHEGRITS
WOWS EBEN VEER
HUE PRELUDETOAKNISH
ITE VANE STEP KAUAI
ZAP THAW EXT OLMOS
```

EVERYBODY LOVES A CLONE

```
TAPS JEDI MESA STP
EDICT IDOL BREW IRA
SUPERBBOWLGAMES DIN
TEENERS NBA INHEELS
EVA SEEPIN URAL
RANIINTERFERENCE
OBI DER IDS OKSANA
DECAL AVON ETS LOX
ELIA ICETRAY ALAI
RUMPPUNCH BAREEXAMS
EGOS GOESFAR TILT
DLV GUN ARES NESTS
SIEGES BAD GUS EAT
ITTAKESAVILLAGE
NARC RAISES TIE
CONDONE TIA BUSPASS
HON MOMAANDAPPLEPIE
USE FLOW TODO ERASE
MEX YARN OGEE SLID
```

FAULTY KEYBOARD

```
WAFT SAMBO GSUITS
ACRO CREEP ELUDER
BLAM RANAT NONONO
CUUMUULUUSCLOUUDS
INB MOP PUB
LUUXUURIOUUS STES
ARF PLANT ACUITY
SIOUX ENT CROUTON
UMASS CHINA
SECRETS PRE KLIEG
AMOUNT SLOES DAN
PERU STUUCKONYOUU
AGS ANG LYE
EPLUURIBUUSUUNUUM
RESUME EGRET TRIO
GLEAMS ALGAE ASEC
STAYAT MYERS SASS
```

ALLOW ME TO INTRODUCE MYSELF

```
SNEER TRASH TWINE
TARTE EIEIO AHOOT
AGATE EBONY HINTS
INSULATINGTAIPEI
NAE WES CTS
GREGORIANCHIANTI
AOKS XOXO WARM
ATASTE LOTION TAP
DELTA TELEX ETAIL
HEE BRAVOS PHILLY
OTRA IBET PORK
CHOCKFULLOINUITS
TEL NEZ WEI
CONNECTTHEIDIOTS
BATIK LURAY AORTA
ALICE ABONE STOLI
RISEN DANDD HAWED
```

CHANGE OF VENUE

```
SNARF  BAN  POL   TAB
LEROI  ELEGANT    HBO
AHAIR  LOVEGODDESS
BILLSOFFARE   OBOL
      TART   MATURE
THIRSTY  REDUCEDBY
RESETS   PETRIE
ARMEE  SOCCER   ODES
COALPITS  HASAMEAL
INNS   ARTIER  DINTY
     AMIENS   TVTIME
SEEDYBARS  CRASSER
ERNIES      COIL
LEIA   WAROPPOSERS
ENGLISHPORT   ROLEO
COM  THEEDGE   ELENA
TWA  SEW  SIR  MOVER
```

```
VENUE
VENUS
MENUS
MINUS
MINES
DINES
DIVES
DOVES
DOVER
MOVER
```

CAN WE TAWK?

```
MASC   ICES   HEATED
ASTA   MARIS  USMINT
ATOB   ARITH  STEALS
MAKINGAQUICKEX
  BENOIT   ELY    ATM
    BON  RELO  LAMIA
SMOKEYANDTHEBAND
AWAY   ART   MARTYS
DIN  PAPERPROF   ETE
AVATAR   AIR    RUIN
GETALEARNERSPERM
ILENE  LETS   EOS
OSE    GOV   TALCUM
   FUHGEDDABOUDIT
CHEAPO   RAIMI   EDDY
COSMOS   BRIER   MEAN
SILENT   KIDD   ERSE
```

COUNTER OFFER

```
MALE   APEMAN   SAGA
ARAL   NEPALI   UKES
HALFINCHCOLDMILK
AMO   NUKE   TENANTS
TALLGLASS    SAT
MILA    TUNE    RAHM
ACORNS   SODAWATER
  GOLF  USNA   TAX
CHOCOLATESYRUP
FRI   KOOL    LENE
LONGSPOON   LETSON
UPTO    DUOS    ACRO
   EEC  STIRAGAIN
TOPSEED   HEAR   LGA
BROOKLYNEGGCREAM
ASOF   ENTREE   HUME
ROLF   BEHELD   EPIS
```

SHORT BREAKS

```
PASTOR   SANITY   ISO
ARLENE   CRECHE   MIN
BMINUSDRIVERS   AGE
LOP   STRIDE  IMIGHT
ORSO  RIP  RELATETO
     ASIF      ALAS
BISECTINGREMARK
ARDENT   SORER   ENT
WIEST   SITED   ASNER
LEA   MANIC   ALKALI
FLAMINGFOOTBALL
     CANT      THAT
ONTHESET  LEE  EAST
BAREST   OSIRIS   FUR
EVA  TRUSTNOSECONE
SEC  RESEAT  TAURUS
ELK  OLEARY  SLEEPS
```

BOUSTROPHEDON

```
YELPS   SCARS   CLEFT
ELOOT   TORAT   AIPES
AMUSEMENTPARKRIDE
   ISPEP    YTLAER
ERSE  APP  AIM   BAS
DEX  DLEIFAGNIWOLP
TVVCR   NOR    XACTO
   RERB  UEIL  SCAT
ONEWAYORANOTHER
ANOW   DERM   EGRU
STREW   IAN   IPASS
NWALEHTGNIWOM  SKO
OOH  BAH   TEM  PHIL
    OCSENE   TNUAH
DOTMATRIXPRINTERS
EVRES   ONADA   ISAUQ
FAINT   NOMSG   TYPES
```

AT ONE'S END'S WIT

```
LAIC   TRACED   ODISTS
ILSA   RETIREE  BANKON
BIER1IMPORTS   INTIME
BETHS     ETA   GOFER
MAYOR  HASACOFFINFIT
ABOO   PARENT   FATE
LAUNCHINTOOBIT  SLUR
   HILO   EXTS   IRE
BRIDAL  LOONEYTOMBS
RUNUP  REXREED  RABAT
IMABEREAVER   MORONS
EON   LEDS    RAIN
FRED  THEBURYINGKIND
  ALAE  ETRADE  ONOR
ONEMEGAHEARSE  TOROS
ROMAN   DAM    MIKAN
GOOGOL  MORGUE&MINDY
ASTERS  STEINEM  EGAD
NEEDED  HONORS   REYS
```

IF I WROTE THE DICTIONARY

```
SORA   SPIN   COOL  CSI
ACES   KOREA  OREO  RAT
LACERATION  MANN  ORA
ARRAU  SCATOLOGICAL
MIO  EKE  ONE  SPLASHY
INSTRUMENTAL    HIT
SASE   DAY   MANIFEST
  COZIEST  TELE  TOW
BASHFUL  TOATEE  HOBO
IDONT   KEDGE   AOLER
ALLO  BRENDA  PILLAGE
SIT   HUEY  SLURRED
  BIBULOUS  KIA  IRMA
ANG   PIGMENTATION
AMALGAM  LII  TED  SNO
DEFIBRILLATE    AHEAD
EDT  AIME  NECROMANCY
PIE  CAEN  TROOP  STAN
TAR  KNOT  SLOT  HONE
```

LIPSTICK ON A PIG

```
AORTAE   CHE   ISS  FAQS
CROATS   RIB  MICROBUS
HAMLOTIONS  OLEOLSEN
ELEM   ASIDE   GINNIE
BOARTOXINJECTIONS
   DIEN    ANO    THE
TROGGS  HOGMENTATION
AIRES   BALE   ADRATE
PEZ   SERENE   ALAI
SNOUTPATIENTSURGERY
  PARK  CREEKS   REV
SONORA   ARMS   TBONE
PLENTYOFSLOP  TARSUS
YOU    PIE    SOLI
FRAGRUNTOINKMENTS
  ORIOLE  SLEET  KOTO
ANTILLES  SOWDOILOOK
MOISTENS   IVE  MTETNA
ONCE    STE   EEL  SAYHEY
```

THE SPORTS BAR

```
PLUS  REB    TIED   HTML
HYPO  ALAS   UNTO   OHIO
DRAFTPICK    STAN   TERI
SANTA SHOTSELECTION
   DERMA KILN  FAUN
SPARTA MIXEDDOUBLES
PIT UNDUE     IRS   AVA
APE FLAT ERMA EDWIN
SEMIFINALROUND  ISLE
   FEE BUILD OSS
LADS RELIEFPITCHERS
ALOOF LESS ASTA  SEA
BOO OIL   VCHIP  PEG
SERVICEBREAK  NUBILE
   POSE EARL  IGLOO
SPLITDECISION  ABNER
TOAD TAOS  UNDERCARD
ALTO ESME  MUIR  AGRA
BEEF AYES   SAG  TESS
```

HOOKED ON HOMOPHONICS

```
ABLE   WARPED   ABRAM
GREW CHRISSIE  GUAVA
NAVELHOSPITAL  ELDER
ACE SAO   ANAT  LIRE
THEWURSTISBEHINDUS
ESSO  HIDE    MOUSE
   LOT SIGN KERR
FIFTYTHOUSANDWHATS
ERR ORA TEASE  AMOO
MEINHARE   PETEMOSS
ISSO ABYSS LAX  RIO
THEHOARSEWHISPERER
   ALLA TAOS ECO
CORGI   ZOIC  MISO
ITMAKESLITTLECENTS
ACID ESAU  IGO  SEW
DETOO THECOMMASUTRA
DRINK EIGHTEEN PEEL
LOSES  BOOSTS  IPOD
```

LETTERHEADS

```
EPEES DINGS   DEADEN
GILDA IDAHO  SERRATE
GPSILOVEYOU  CPRFIRM
SEAT BAA STRAP   LEO
   OWENS THOR  TRY
SUVRAYS  SPFCHANGS
CHEST  CASEY  HETERO
OUGHT SHULA  ALLEWIS
THAI  POLO BROM  SPA
   PBJANDTHEBEAR
NAP RANG CODY   AJAR
OLEMISS SALES  ADAGE
VIRAGO JCREW    NIVEN
ATVDINNER   OCDCASE
   ADD ALUM FREYA
VAS  BILBO AGO  LANA
CGIBILL BMXMISSILES
REVOKES EMCEE  OZARK
SEEPED  RAIDS  BENDS
```

SAY WHAT?

```
CAPTCHA SCRIMP  APPL
ABRAHAM TAIPEI  SARA
SEIKODEFENDANT  AYES
ATM RAND TED  IMPROV
   DUC REB DEE  AWE
ANBESOL SEIJISTRING
MOET WONK COP  ATSEA
ADLAI BAITERS  LEEDS
SALINEONME  JOEL
STALAG NORMA  RIGSUP
   POKY SAFERCOATS
PARTI ACTEDON  ATRIA
ONEBC RAE EXES  HALL
SAJAKHAMMER  STEINEM
TOO LAT FAA    ENC
GRIMES IMF DIET  AKA
ATCO SADIECOMPOSING
MIEN LIEDTO  ELMTREE
EZRA EDDIES  DEBASED
```

WILD KINGDOM

```
ASTRIDE ITASCA GOSPEL
MARINES MOTHER INHALE
ETONCAP BITEOFFTHERAT
COUGAR LILI AMBIENT
HUTS TRIBECA CROOK
ETS WHALETAGGER DIME
CORSET EAR FLORET
TROPE CLANOFTHEMOTH
ACORNS GOOUT YAW NAY
PAPA OPERAS DPS IDYLL
HADESOFTHELOUSE
ABYSM ATT RERUNS AGRA
DOA ESC SIRES AIROUT
DOTINTHESHARK NIOBE
TRENDY PEI COAXES
OSSA BEAVERWORDS ESS
CADRE AQUINAS ASTA
SHATNER USES PALLOR
HIDINGRABBITS PAGEANT
OLIVIA COUPLE SCEPTER
DONEES HANSEL SEEHERE
```

WHERE OH WHERE?

```
MISTER◊ RATSO TALBOT
ANTONIO IDEALS EMILIO
STEPSON DENTAL MODELT
SETOUT GET◊FORPUSH◊S
ELSUR ITEMS AON
TENSE EXITSTAGE◊
RAP ANTSY VENI SWAMI
ISAIDSO TABASCO ELIS
SYNCED JOKES DESERT
ELIEL SEGUE FELIX
◊ACREEKWITHOUTAPADDLE
TEASE IBEAM CIAOS
DAMSEL OVERT STAMOS
ITSA OLDWEST ◊TOLIFE
GEEKS ZEAL EERIE NAS
◊◊CITIZENS PERMA
ASI EDAMS ALAMO
◊FORTHEWOLVES SLOGAN
TAPOUT ALIOTO GILMORE
AMENRA SICKEN OCEANIA
BESSER DEERE ◊STREAM
```

ADDITIONAL CAST

```
FLOWERS CHAD PAD EWE
RANALONG RULE ORE LEA
AMERICANFORALLSEASONS
NAM SPARS SIMIANCITY
CRISP SWASH ANTS ASIA
NUIT MTA LENS
DOUBTABLEINDEMNITY
OATH LOIRE ELAYNE RIB
TREE LOPS ONENESS AGE
ALOT LUIGI LOGON
DUDEWHERESMYCADAVER
BURST VENTS BOSE
RAG SPREADS BEAR RCMP
ALE BIERCE TALCS HAIR
MEETTHEPARLIAMENTS
LALA OLE LOAD
ITON NACL PIXEL PRISM
BOUNDERDOG SADAT DUO
INVADERSFROMMASONJARS
DEE ADO TINA MEDIATES
ORR YAW SPAN ROBBERY
```

HEADS OF STATE

```
GULAGS MISSA FASTPACE
ADAGIO OAKEN DIORAMAS
PAPERFORMING ARTISANS
ELS LAHR TOLD THAT
SLEW MISTRESSRELATED
ONE ELIA CHARS AXE
ALEVELS ASST AVE GLUT
COVERMOUTH EAVE ERODE
TREND TRE CAMELSDINER
INN ETD SORE AIM
VAINGLOURIOUSBASTERDS
OIL ONKP USE ORO
MOROSEMARIE GOT EBSEN
AHOST AMYS MAYOADRIAN
CALE DDE ETAL ROGUERY
ARE BUENO REOS KEN
WAXMARKSTHESPOT OLAY
ORAN TOAT MUFF ALE
IHOPENOT SCRAMBLINMAN
TAKESTWO ELOPE ASSERT
SMARTENS RESTS PHARMA
```

KANGAROO PHRASES

```
BEN STOA GNOTE IMCOLD
WRECKERS OHBOY NAUSEA
ISRAELIAIRLINE THREAD
DRE ROGETS ERASERS
TWITTERUSERSUPDATE
RHEE SAL ROI MACAU
AES SATELLITEOFSATURN
PETROL IONA FYI RTE
AHEM MANIA COLA
JORDANADOLLAR LICKS
IVANV LVI LAO ICAME
MAGEE LATENIGHTTVHOST
TRIO ERATO SOIE
PSI DIE DIAN TENDON
SIMPSONSBARTENDER IKE
TREAT EEE IER LEIA
PURPLERAINCOMPOSER
FEARNOT PARSEE ARI
LATINO CIRCLEDSQUARES
EVOKES SNIDE ONELLAMA
DEPART AGNES GODS ETC
```

AT LAST!

```
TACOMA ASSUMES REAMS
AMORAL ALAMODE YELLAT
POWERSTHATBEAT AFLAME
IRE KOR NIE MIDDLECAT
NERDS ALTERS NODE ABS
AMANA TOP LAX REO
YOUTALKINTOMEAT STAN
ABSENT LOA APB USHER
PLED DART TURNTO
PAR MHO MAMMOTHCAVEAT
EDITIONS MAE SOLVENCY
RIDINGHABITAT NEE TAP
RIGOUR NOTE JODI
DRESS DUB TRU ARAMIS
BEES FINETOOTHCOMBAT
AFL CHI OAR SAHIB
SIE HARK MIDAIR DAMPS
SANTAFEAT GOP DER ELI
INTENT BOARDINGPASSAT
SCENES UKRAINE IGUANA
TEDDY LETMEGO CENSOR
```

THE LONG AND THE SHORT OF IT

```
DEAN ABOIL JAVA UHF
JOKES LANCE EPIC ORAL
SNACKSINTHEGRACE CATO
TIP DAD OKRA SANTA
ALPACAS PINESTRIPSUIT
BEARARMS EAT REESES
REC PEAKONTHECHECK
ARIAS SYD ETHOS SOY
DENS OHYEAH HAH INURE
EDGIER SUBARU MEMES
GAMOFKATEANDMOUSE
BURNT ALLAYS ASTROS
AMASS RIB SHOWER ESPY
MAD SINES PAL WAKEN
SITSEEINGTRIPE UNO
SPLICE RYE STUBBLED
WHOLEWETBREED ENFOLDS
OILED JOIE KAN CEO
OLIN TENDERIZETHEKNIT
PITT OCTO DEERE TIARA
SPA ETON ARSON EGAD
```

GENDER BENDER

```
AWFUL ALAS VEGAN
PARSE CINE MILANO
ONION HEYADECIMAL
PET SUES WEAK
OVENS HARRISON
PELOSI WIVES PTAS
BNAI SIRE RAISE
SEXCHANGE ADA CAT
EUROS OMEGA
AHA RIB OPERATION
BAGEL PAIN EDNA
CLUE TRITE TRAITS
SANDWICH BROMO
OINK IAIM TBA
BRANDXGLASS ALBUM
REBOOT ERIE NAOMI
ODETS SEND ABYSS
```

UP-SCALE

```
ASSERTS URGE JOGS
LETSOUT LOOM ELLE
ECOTONE MUSCLEDOC
RENEDEAL THEOREMS
ODE MALI ETE
SEDATE MINTSTRIKE
LISTENER OSCAR
FALLSTONE ASS APT
AMIS EMT GWU TRUE
TAN WEB SOLDDIETS
ANDSO ASSASSIN
LAOCONCERT YESMEN
ADO ASIP ANT
SKELETAL TIPDANCE
HARDDOMES NEONGAS
ELIE NOGS TAUTEST
DEED ERST ASPIRES
```

SUB-MERGING

W	A	T	E	R	S	K	I		A	N	A		O	I	L	Y
C	R	A	Y	O	N	E	D		T	O	T	A	L	D	U	E
S	I	D	E	W	A	Y	S		A	W	A	R	D	I	N	G
		L	A	K	E			T	I	R	E		G	A	G	
M	A	R	I	N	E	D	I	V	I	S	I	O	N			
A	L	A	N	S		P	I	L	E			O	K	R	A	
D	U	N	E		Z	E	R	O	T	R	A	C	T	I	O	N
	M	A	R	G	I	N	A	L		U	R	A	N	U	S	
B	I	N		O	N	L	Y		S	O	N	E		G	S	A
A	N	A	L	O	G			M	O	N	T	E	R	O	S	
H	U	M	A	N	S	P	E	C	I	E	S		E	T	E	S
A	M	E	R		O	N	C	D				S	S	T	A	R
		C	L	A	S	S	C	O	N	S	C	I	O	U	S	
I	D	I		I	M	I	N			O	A	R	S			
N	O	N	G	R	A	T	A		O	R	B	I	T	G	U	M
S	E	T	O	R	D	E	R		C	A	R	P	O	R	T	S
T	R	O	D		O	D	E		T	H	E	T	R	E	E	S

YOU'RE SOLVING . . . WITH WHAT?

A	S	H	R	A	M	S		R	A	I	N	S		S	R	S
C	H	A	I	T	E	A		E	P	S	O	N		L	A	C
C	O	N	F	O	R	M		P	A	T	R	O	N	I	Z	E
T	A	N	T	E		O	N	E	I	L		W	E	W	O	N
S	L	A	V		U	S	E	G	R	E	A	T	C	A	R	E
			A	N	T	A	E				P	I	K			
E	T	A	L	I	A		J	A	W	E	R		S	R	O	
S	A	I	L	T	H	R	O	U	G	H		E	Q	U	A	L
S	I	T	E		N	I	N	N	I	E	S		U	Z	I	S
E	N	C	Y	C		F	A	I	N	T	P	R	A	I	S	E
N	T	H		O	N	E	N	O		A	I	L	E	E	N	
			P	I	E			H	A	N	O	I				
F	L	Y	I	N	G	C	O	L	O	R	S		F	U	L	L
A	E	O	N	S		A	W	A	R	E		T	Y	P	E	O
K	I	D	G	L	O	V	E	S		T	H	E	F	L	O	W
I	C	E		O	V	E	N	S		H	E	R	O	I	N	E
R	A	L		T	O	R	S	O		A	B	O	R	T	E	D

CROSSOVER HITS

S	A	H	I	B		S	T	A	R			S	K	I	M	P
C	L	I	M	E		H	U	L	A	S		T	A	H	O	E
H	A	P	P	Y	T	O	G	E	T	H		E	R	O	S	E
W	I	P	E	O	U	T		T	E	R	M	P	A	P	E	R
A	N	O	I	N	T		S	A	D	I	E		T	E	S	S
				C	T	R	L		G	N	A	T				
I	M	A	B	E	L	I	E	V		E	R	G	R	E	E	N
D	I	R	E		E	P	E	E	S		A	I	E	L	L	O
E	A	R	N	S		S	T	R	E	P		F	A	C	E	S
A	T	O	N	O	F		S	N	E	A	K		C	I	N	E
L	A	Z	Y	B	O	N		E	S	W	E	E	T	D	A	Y
				S	L	A	G			A	L	E	C			
A	T	M	S		I	N	L	A	W		N	O	F	U	S	S
R	E	E	N	A	C	T	O	R		J	O	C	A	S	T	A
D	R	E	A	M		E	R	I	C	A	N	I	D	I	O	T
O	S	S	I	E		S	I	E	U	R		D	E	N	N	Y
R	E	E	L	S			A	S	P	S		E	D	G	E	R

GOING UNDERGROUND

I	N	C	O	L	O	R		V	A	C			T	B	A	R
N	E	A	R	Y	O	U		I	R	M	A		H	A	L	E
T	H	E	D	E	F	I		S	E	A	S	N	A	K	E	S
L	I	N	E			Z	A	H	N		S	U	T	U	R	E
			R	A	T		S	N	O	R	T	S		L	O	T
E	D	K	O	C	H		A	U	T	O			M	A	S	S
L	I	E	U	T	E	N			O	N	E	S				
I	C	E	T		C	E	A	S	E		I	M	G	O	O	D
T	E	N		G	O	B	A	N	A	N	A	S		P	A	W
E	Y	E	S	U	P		H	O	T	E	L		L	I	K	E
			I	N	S	T			C	O	L	O	N	E	L	
W	E	I	R		H	A	U	S		N	U	G	E	N	T	
I	N	F		S	P	U	R	N	S			G	I	G		
N	O	F	A	I	R		C	I	T	E		E	B	A	Y	
G	R	I	N	N	E	D	A	T		P	U	D	D	I	N	G
I	M	E	D		T	U	D	E		P	R	I	O	R	T	O
T	E	R	I		B	E	D		S	L	E	N	D	E	R	

TAKE FIVE

H	I	N	D	U		M	O	L	T		R	A	M	M	E	D
O	N	I	O	N		U	N	T	O		E	L	A	I	N	E
W	T	C	H	S	C	L	D	R	N		C	A	T	N	I	P
E	L	K		T	H	E	O		I	S	A		C	O	A	T
			A	R	E		P	S	C	P	L	C	H	R	C	H
E	A	S	Y	A		S	E	T		A	L	O	G			
G	S	L	N	P	M	P		E	E	N		G	A	B	L	E
B	E	E		S	O	A	K	I	N		U	S	M	A	I	L
E	V	E	L		D	S	C	N	T	R	T		E	R	M	A
R	E	V	E	R	E		A	F	R	A	I	D		B	I	P
T	R	E	M	E		O	R	E		J	L	R	B	R	T	S
			O	A	T	S		L	A	A		E	R	A	S	E
P	L	T	N	M	B	L	N	D	S		J	A	R			
S	O	U	P		O	O	O		I	K	I	D		C	G	I
H	A	T	E	O	N		F	N	D	N	G	F	T	H	R	S
A	T	T	E	N	D		E	P	E	E		U	H	A	U	L
W	H	I	L	E	S		E	R	S	E		L	E	T	B	E

SOLUTIONS
Round 4: PLAYOFFS

TESTING, TESTING, 1, 2, 3 . . .

```
C A P I T A L G ■ ■ G A S P A R
O R A T O R I O ■ A L P I N E
W I N S G O L D ■ S T U N T S
S A G A ■ M A S S M A R K E T
■ ■ B E A C H P A R T Y ■ ■
T B I L L S ■ I R I S ■ R E B
B A S A L ■ U P O N ■ D I C E
O N A S S I S ■ U S T I N O V
N E A T ■ M O L T ■ E A G L E
E S C ■ C A P O ■ H A N S E L
■ S T O L E N B A S E ■ ■
H A T E M O N G E R ■ T E R M
I B E X E S ■ B R A S I L I A
P I R A T E ■ O N S E C O N D
S E N S O R ■ W E S T S I D E
```

LANGUAGE IMMERSION

```
L E A S H ■ W I S E S U P T O
E M C E E ■ I N T R U S I O N
F E R A L ■ E Q U I V O Q U E
T R O L L ■ N U N S ■ U G H
J I B ■ S T E I N ■ O M A H A
A T A ■ C I R R I ■ R A N I N
B I T M A P ■ E N L I S T E D
■ E N U F ■ G E E S ■ ■
M I S T Y P E D ■ G N E I S S
I N T R O ■ N I P A T ■ N E E
T A K E N ■ C A R L A ■ J A N
C H I ■ D E L I ■ L I E N S
H O T H E A D E D ■ R O C C O
U L T R A N I C E ■ U T T E R
M E S S T E N T S ■ G A S S Y
```

ROUTE 66

```
C A S T L E ■ C A S H C R O P
A N T H E M ■ A L K A L I N E
M I R A G E ■ P L A Y A C T S
E M I N O R ■ G E T S M A R T
R A K E ■ G A U G E ■ B R I E
A T E ■ P E N N E ■ C E D A R
S E R P E N T S ■ C A R O L S
■ R A C E ■ R O S E ■ ■
M U T E L Y ■ M I L K D U D S
U N I T S ■ B O N E S ■ P U P
G A T E ■ M A N G A ■ H A R E
S W A N S O N G ■ D O O H A N
H A N D I T T O ■ E X T E N D
O R I E N T A L ■ R E L A T E
T E A R O O M S ■ S N Y D E R
```

TALENT SHOW

```
B A M B I ■ C H E S S G A M E
O N I O N ■ A I R Q U O T E S
S A X O N ■ S T R U M P E T S
S L I M E ■ T H A I S ■ C H A
M O T ■ R E S E N D ■ P R A Y
A G U A ■ L O R D ■ K R O N E
N Y P D B L U E ■ S T E W E D
■ A L I T ■ A U E L ■ ■
P R A G U E ■ S R I L A N K A
R A R E R ■ P A R T ■ W E T S
O P T S ■ G O W E S T ■ B O P
T I F ■ B O M B S ■ A G U S H
E D I T E D O U T ■ N I L L A
A L L A T O N C E ■ G M A I L
M Y M I S T A K E ■ S P E N T
```

WELL-CONNECTED

```
G E A R E D U P ■ S E V E R E
U P T O D A T E ■ U N I T A S
N O T M Y D E P A R T M E N T
I D E A S ■ T U G S ■ R D A
T E N N ■ S C A L E ■ K N O T
■ T O E H O L D ■ S H A M E
D P I ■ P O L K ■ I T A L I C
I R O N O U T ■ S P I N O Z A
G O N E X T ■ W E A N ■ P E R
I M P L Y ■ L E T S E A T ■
T I L L ■ G O T H S ■ V I S E
A S E ■ W I G S ■ R A M O N
L E A D A D O U B L E L I F E
I M S O L D ■ I M A L O S E R
S E E M L Y ■ T W O O N T W O
```

IT COMES DOWN TO THIS

```
S U P E R P A C ■ I N C A P S
K R A T I O N S ■ D O L L O P
I I S A M U E L ■ S T A P L E
R A T ■ A R M E D ■ A S H E N
T H E M ■ I W O N ■ S A D D
■ O R D A I N E R ■ G A L
I A M T O O ■ S U R E ■ E N E
T H E H U L K ■ T V E X E C S
T A M ■ S L I M ■ E V O K E S
I M O ■ H A R A S S E R ■
C O R A ■ R O T C ■ Y A W N
K M A R T ■ V I O L A ■ L E A
L E N D E R ■ S T A M P A C T
E N D O R A ■ S C R E A M A T
S T A R R Y ■ E H A R M O N Y
```

FITTING WORDS

```
S N A P B R I M ■ C H A C H A
N A Z A R E N E ■ O O D L E S
I S U R E C A N ■ I N S E R T
F A R M T O T A B L E ■ A B U
F L E A ■ U R G E S ■ G R I D
■ S P I E L ■ H A L V E
F A N A T I C S ■ S I M E O N
A P O L U N E ■ W A L M A R T
T H R O N G ■ B A L L A D E S
A R E N T ■ C E R E S ■ ■
L O G E ■ C R A M S ■ C A F E
F D R ■ Y O U R E T H E M A N
L I E N O R ■ I D E A L I Z E
A T T I R E ■ S T A T E G E M
W E S L E Y ■ H O M E B O D Y
```

FINAL EXAM

```
S L U G A B E D S ■ S T O M P
P A N A S O N I C ■ C A P R I
L U M P S U G A R ■ A D E P T
I R A S ■ G I L E A D ■ N E S
F E D ■ T H R O W N ■ S W A T
F L E S H ■ D U C K ■ W I N O
■ H I S ■ T A L K E D U P
S T L U C I A ■ P E L L E T S
C R O C K E T T ■ S A L ■
R I S K ■ S L O B ■ U S E R S
A M E S ■ T A P I N S ■ S E P
B A H ■ D A N G L E ■ S A M E
B R O K E ■ T E L L S A L I E
L A P I N ■ I A M L E G E N D
E N E M Y ■ C R E S C E N D O
```

1. TO TELL THE TRUTH

```
NEAT  SPADE  QUAD
EXGI  TIDAL  URGE
OPENSESAME   ANON
SODAS  ARENAS
       FRANKSINATRA
MODEST       TRIES
OPRY  HARASS  EDS
STY  HONESTY  ROI
AID  ELISHA  BONG
IMEAN      GOLDEN
CANDIDCAMERA
    DEARME  ESSAY
PETS  REALESTATE
BEAU  LATER  ETON
SLOP  AMIES  DEMS
```

2. FIVE BOROUGH BRIDGES

```
CURFEW  DAH  ACCOST
USAUSA  JAI  NOIDEA
BATMAN  HAT  TANDEM
EIS  INGE  ISIS  ESP
SNOB  AERATE  TASTE
    LEBRON  XFACTOR
LEGUME   OCTILE
ATARI  SOSOON   AWE
HOLBROOK  LYNCHPIN
RNS  ARLISS  ZORRO
   TEHRAN  BASSES
OBLIQUE  ENSURE
AEIOU  LAZIER  ARCH
TNT  ASSN  SAGA  ALA
ESTATE  NIS  LANDON
ROLLON  IDA  ERRAND
SNEERS  EON  SPARKY
```

3. SILENCE OF THE LAMPREYS

```
BOSS  JAMB   SSR  AHAB
EDIT  IMOUT  ATE  TADA
NONE  FIXTHECAT  HMOS
TREVI   ITAL  RAVEL
   WINGWESTVIRGINIA
THALIA   SEC  CASTS
SRO  ERICS  RHODA  COO
COURTOFAPPS   DERSHIP
APSES  RUE  RINSE
BEER  THERTHING  TONI
 ABOUT  ROD  AARON
RYANOWN  CAUGHTSTING
OUR  UNGER  REAPS  GEE
ORMAN   MOW   WEEBIT
 THECAPTAINANDTEN
  ONEIR  KNOT  SCARF
FILE  LOOSEBALL  OLIO
IKEA  EVA  SERTA  OLDE
BESS  YET  LIDS  LYES
```

4. SPACED OUT

```
MADAM  CASTS   RAW
AROMA  LAURA   ETA
GREENHORNET   TAX
   LIEGE  PIERRE
LABIALS  SIRLOIN
ENLACE  OHDEAR
ANA  SNARE  STOWS
POCK  ALIEN  ECHO
TYKES  TONIC  KOP
 MACRON  POMELO
SWATHES  SPOUTER
PERSON  WEEKS
OAK  ONTHEDOCKET
IVE  LEVER  FLORA
LET  STAYS  FEIGN
```

5. SEND IN THE CLONES

```
INCA  CTSCAN  UMBER
MELD  OHMAGE  PARLE
GUESTHOUSES  SKOAL
ARA  HOUDIN  HEALY
MOTORS  GOT  ROAD
ENSUE  WES  LETSEAT
  TECH  RUNSINTO
WBC  PROTRACT  FIRM
AAH  MARRAKESH  NIM
SHIM  CLEMENTE  GAY
PANCAKES   COLE
SICKBED  TEY  OUIJA
 HEAD  PES  AIRMEN
CHILL  ATHENS  PEG
HULLO  STRANGELOVE
ARLEN  HEARYE  USER
PLANE  OLDPAL  MESS
```

6. UH . . . LIKE . . . YOU KNOW?

```
RAHRAH  DEARSIRS  SUP
ONETWO  ALLEYOOP  CPA
MOMENTUMOFTRUTH  ION
ASPS  OPENS   EVENT
   DISS  OATBRAN
PROFILE  BIBLEBELTER
RANIS  TRADEINS  LILO
ORELSE  ORLY  JESSA
MEDIUMCARE  SPRAYTAN
 BAALS   ORANG
ONBUDGET  OFFERSIDES
NORSE   ARIA  APRILS
ATIT  SUBGENRE  OLMAN
NINEMUSEUMS  MORSELS
 GRENADE   SENT
RAISA   ESTEE  SISI
ART  NEWYORKERGIANTS
NEO  IVEEATEN  ORIGIN
DAN  TEATREES  DESERT
```

7. IT ALL ADDS UP

```
MAILBAG  MESS  ARD  SMOG
ASTORIA   ALTO  REALTIME
THENUMBERSIN  MANIACAL
SERENA  EVERYCOLUMNAND
     CTRL   LIMBO
OOMPH  HEADGEAR  ESSMAN
THAI  DODGEASPEN  HALE
TAGGER  TEMP  CHEATER
ARI  LOUD  PEN  TOOLSHED
WAC  MOTEL672ON  MITE
ASST  PAGE159HOLE  AMPS
 QUAI  AT834STARS  ALA
HAUNTERS  ICE  EMUS  TAY
ELANTRA  RAYS  NEWISH
MERE  MAJORETTES  ACME
PRELAW  WINDSURF  ESSAY
  SICEM   ASIA
DIAGONALANDROW  DREDGE
ENVELOPE  TOTALFIFTEEN
ECOTOURS  STET  INUTERO
MANS  TIS  BOSS  SALUTES
```

Will Shortz is the crossword editor of the
New York Times, founder and director of the
American Crossword Puzzle Tournament, and the
puzzlemaster for NPR's *Weekend Edition Sunday*.
He lives in Pleasantville, New York.